THE ROYAL COURT THEAT

CW00551713

Cuckoo

by Michael Wynne

Cuckoo was first performed at the Royal Court Jerwood Theatre
Downstairs, Sloane Square, on Thursday 6 July 2023.

Cuckoo
by Michael Wynne

Cast

Carmel **Michelle Butterly**
Megyn **Emma Harrison**
Doreen **Sue Jenkins**
Sarah **Jodie McNee**

Director **Vicky Featherstone**
Designer **Peter McKintosh**
Lighting Designer **Jai Morjaria**
Sound Designer & Composer **Nick Powell**
Movement Director **Jonnie Riordan**
Assistant Director **Jade Franks**
Associate Lighting Designer **Tom Turner**
Deputy Stage Manager **Katie Stephen**
Assistant Stage Manager **Lottie Denby**
Sound Operator **Florence Hand**
Set built by **Ridiculous Solutions**

From the Royal Court, on this production:

Casting Directors **Amy Ball & Arthur Carrington**
Stage Supervisor **Steve Evans**
Lead Producer **Sarah Georgeson**
Production Manager **Marius Rønning**
Lighting Programmer **Stephen Settle**
Company Stage Manager **Mica Taylor**
Lighting Supervisor **Deanna Towli**
Costume Supervisor **Lucy Walshaw**

Cuckoo has been generously supported by a lead gift from Charles Holloway.
Further support has been received by members of the Cuckoo Production Circle.
It is produced in association with Liverpool Everyman & Playhouse.

Michael Wynne (Writer)

Michael is a playwright and screenwriter Cuckoo is his 8th play for the Royal Court.

For the Royal Court: **I'm Not Here – Living Newspaper Edition 4, Who Cares, The Red Flag, Friday Night Sex [with Alecky Blythe], The Priory, The People Are Friendly, The Knocky.**

Other theatre includes: **We Are Here (La Mama, New York); The Star (Liverpool Playhouse); Hope Place (Liverpool Everyman); Collider (Science Museum/Nissen Richards Studio); Canvas (Minerva Theatre, Chichester); Tits/Teeth (NYT/Soho); Dirty Wonderland, Sell Out (Frantic Assembly); The Boy Who Left Home (ATC/Lyric Hammersmith); Too Cold for Snow (The Prada Foundation).**

Television includes: **Being Eileen, Lapland, Little Crackers: The Daltons/Sheridan Smith, The Catherine Tate Show, Eastenders, The Gil Mayo Mysteries, Sugar Rush, Eyes Down, As If, UGetMe, Don't Eat the Neighbours, Reach for the Moon, Grafters, Where the Heart is.**

Film includes: **My Summer of Love.**

Awards include: **BAFTA for Outstanding British Film (My Summer of Love); Evening Standard Award for Best Screenplay (My Summer of Love); Olivier Award for Best New Comedy (The Priory); Meyer Whitworth Award for Best New Play (The Knocky).**

Michelle Butterly (Carmel)

For the Royal Court: **The People Are Friendly.**

Other theatre includes: **Betty! A Sort Of Musical, A Streetcar Named Desire, Hamlet (Manchester Royal Exchange); The Last Testament Of Lillian Bilocca (The Guildhall, Hull); Everyman (National) The Star, Hope Place, Dead Heavy Fantastic (Liverpool Everyman); Blair's Children (Cockpit); One For The Road (Royal & Derngate Theatre, Northampton); Gaslight (Theatre Clwyd); Road (Wolsey Theatre, Ipswich); Queen Of The Nile (Hull Truck Theatre); I Like Mine With A Kiss (Bush); Ma Vie en Rose (Young Vic); Gone To Earth (Lyric Hammersmith); Laundry Room At The Hotel Madrid (Gate); Noughts And Crosses, A New Way To Please You, Believe What You Will, Speaking Like Magpies, A Servant to Two Masters (& Young Vic/West End), Thomas More (RSC).**

Television includes: **Craith, Anthony, Little Boy Blue, McMafia, Benidorm, Beautiful People, Midsummers Murders, Minder, No Angels, Eyes Down, Casualty, Dangerfield, Pie in the Sky, Hetty Wainthrop Investigates, Soldier Soldier.**

Lottie Denby
(Assistant Stage Manager)

For the Royal Court: **Jews. In Their Own Words, Living Archive, two Palestinians go dogging [SM Placement].**

Other theatre includes: **The Three Billy Goats Gruff, Anansi the Spider (Unicorn); Dear Santa (Chichester Festival/Leicester Curve); Cinderella (Stratford East).**

Opera includes: **La Bohème (Nevill Holt Opera).**

Vicky Featherstone (Director)

For the Royal Court: **all of it, Jews. In Their Own Words., The Glow, Maryland, Living Newspaper, Shoe Lady, On Bear Ridge (& National Theatre Wales) [co-director], Cyprus Avenue (& Abbey, Dublin/MAC, Belfast/Public, NYC), The Cane, Gundog, My Mum's a Twat, Bad Roads, Victory Condition, X, How to Hold Your Breath, God Bless the Child, Maidan: Voices from the Uprising, The Mistress Contract, The Ritual Slaughter of Gorge Mastromas; Untitled Matriarch Play, The President Has Come to See You (Open Court Weekly Rep).**

Other theatre includes: **What if Women Ruled the World? (Manchester International Festival); Our Ladies of Perpetual Succour (& National/ West End/International tour), Enquirer [co director], An Appointment with the Wicker Man, 27, The Wheel, Somersaults, Wall of Death: A Way of Life [co-director], The Miracle Man, Empty, Long Gone Lonesome (National Theatre of Scotland); Cockroach (National Theatre of Scotland/Traverse); 365 (National Theatre of Scotland/Edinburgh International Festival); Mary Stuart (National Theatre of Scotland/ Citizens/Royal Lyceum, Edinburgh); The Wolves in the Walls [co-director] (National Theatre of Scotland/Tramway/Lyric, Hammersmith/ UK tour/New Victory, NYC); The Small Things, Pyrenees, On Blindness, The Drowned World, Tiny Dynamite, Crazy Gary's Mobile Disco, Splendour, Riddance, The Cosmonaut's Last Message to the Woman He Once Loved in the Former Soviet Union, Crave (Paines Plough).**

Television includes: **Pritilata (from Snatches: Moments from 100 Years of Women's Lives), Where the Heart is, Silent Witness.**

Vicky was Artistic Director of Paines Plough 1997-2005 and the inaugural Artistic Director of the National Theatre of Scotland 2005-2012. She is the Artistic Director of the Royal Court.

Jade Franks (Assistant Director)

As an actor, for the Royal Court: **One Night Stand, Maryland.**

As assistant director, theatre includes: **OV Theatre Makers (The Old Vic)**

As an actor, other theatre includes: **Hot in Here (Gate/Pigfoot); Run, Painkiller, Slambition (Theatre Royal Stratford East).**

Emma Harrison (Megyn)

Emma recently graduated from the Royal Central School of Speech and Drama. This is Emma's professional debut.

Sue Jenkins (Doreen)

For the Royal Court: **The People are Friendly.**

Other theatre includes: **Maybe Tomorrow (Royal Exchange); The Changeling (Contact Theatre); The Price (Library Theatre Company); 20th Century Boy (Bolanic Productions); The Vagina Monologues (Mark Goucher Ltd); Wizard of Oz (The Lowry); School For Wives, The Devils, Educating Rita, Tom Jones (Leeds Playhouse); Othello, As You Like It, Twelfth Night (Bolton Octagon).**

Television includes: **Doctor Who, It's a Sin, Home from Home, Being Eileen, It's Okay to be Ray, Heartbeat, Midsomer Murders, Dalziel and Pasco, The Beiderbecke Affair, The Girls Who Came to Stay, The Royal, In Deep, Casualty, Doctors, Coasting, Holby City, How We Used To Live, Brookside, In Suspicious Circumstances, Coronation Street.**
Radio includes: **Over 250 radio plays, audio books, stories & classic adaptations including Wuthering Heights, Middlemarch, Villette, The Citadel, A Clockwork Orange.**

Film includes: **Blue Collars and Buttercups.**

Peter McKintosh (Designer)

For the Royal Court: **The Heretic.**

Other theatre includes: **4000 Miles, South Pacific (& Sadlers Wells/UK tour), Shadowlands, Guys And Dolls, Uncle Vanya, Antony And Cleopatra, Love Story , Pal Joey (Chichester Festival); Trouble in Butetown, St Nicholas, The York Realist, The Resistable Rise Of Arturo Ui, Serenading Louie, Splendour, My Night With Reg (& Apollo), Luise Miller, The Chalk Garden, John Gabriel Borkman, Boston Marriage (& West End), The Cryptogram (Donmar); Relatively Speaking (& UK tour), The Realistic Joneses, God of Carnage, Hay Fever (Theatre Royal Bath); 42nd Street (Theatre du Chatelet); Orlando (Garrick); All My Sons, Twelve Angry Men (Theatre Cocoon, Tokyo); After The End, Shining City, Extinct, The Sun The Moon And**

Stars, King Hedley II (Stratford East); Funny Girl, Guys And Dolls (Marigny); A Day In The Death Of Joe Egg (Trafalgar); , On The Town, Seven Brides For Seven Brothers, The Sound Of Music, Crazy For You (& West End), Hello Dolly! (Regents Park Open Air); The Doctor's Dilemma, Our Country's Good, Widowers' Houses, Honk! (National); Macbeth (Globe); The Wind In The Willows (Palladium/UK tour); Guys and Dolls, Dirty Rotten Scoundrels (& UK tour) (West End/Savoy); The Importance Of Being Earnest (West End/Vaudeville/UK tour); The Winslow Boy (& Roundabout, New York), Noises Off (& Novello/UK tour) (Old Vic); Viva Forever!, Death And The Maiden, Butley, Entertaining Mr Sloane, Prick Up Your Ears, The Dumb Waiter, Fiddler On The Roof, King John, Summer And Smoke, Donkey's Years, The Birthday Party, The Home Place, Brand, A Woman Of No Importance (West End); The Turn Of The Screw, The Knot Of The Heart, Waste, Cloud Nine, Romance (Almeida); Apologia (Bush); 39 Steps (Broadway/World tour/West End); Kirikou Et Karaba (Casino de Paris/Maison de la Danse/French tour); The Black Dahlia (Yale Repertory Company); Romeo and Juliet (Shakespeare Theatre, Washington DC); Alice in Wonderland, King John, Pericles, Brand (& West End) The Merry Wives of Windsor (RSC).

Opera includes: **The Marriage of Figaro (English National Opera); The Handmaid's Tale (Royal Danish Opera/ English National Opera/ Canadian Opera); Hansel And Gretel (Regents Park Open Air).**

Peter received the Olivier Award for Best Costume Design (Crazy For You).

Peter is a founder member of Freelancers Make Theatre Work.

Jodie McNee (Sarah)

For the Royal Court: **Anatomy of a Suicide, Maryland.**

Other theatre includes: **Orlando (MGC); Adult Children (Donmar); Faustus That Damned Woman (Headlong); Nora A Doll's House, The Night Watch, Hamlet, Orpheus Descending, A Taste of Honey (Royal Exchange, Manchester); An Oak Tree, Our Country's Good, Three Winters (National); Game (Almeida); Venice Preserved, A Life of Galileo, Written on the Heart, Measure for Measure (RSC); Hobson's Choice (Regent's Park Open Air); My White Best Friend, Canary, When We Are Married, Twelfth Night (Liverpool Everyman Playhouse); The Empty Quarter (Hampstead); When We are Married (West End); The Frontline, King Lear (Globe); Seagull, Knives in Hens, Double Portrait, Jenufer (Arcola); Cymbeline, The Changeling (Cheek by Jowl/Barbican/International tour); Mother Courage, This Happy Breed (ETT); The Burial at Thebes (Playhouse, Nottingham).**

Television includes: **Breathtaking, Mrs Sidhu Investigates, Culprits, Hollington Drive, Anthony, Unprecedented/Fear Fatigue, Britannia 1-3, Agatha and the Midnight Murders, Vera, Little Boy Blue, Ripper Street, Criminal Justice, Poirot.**

Film includes: **Judy, Official Secrets, Film Stars Don't Die in Liverpool, The Physician, Collider, One Happy Moment, A Picture of Me.**

Radio includes: **The American Grandmother, Zola: Blood Season, With Great Pleasure.**

Jai Morjaria (Lighting Designer)

For the Royal Court: **Graceland.**

Other theatre includes: **Othello (National); The Trials (Donmar); My Son's A Queer (But What Can You Do?) (Ambassadors/Garrick/Underbelly/Turbine); Chasing Hares (Young Vic); Wuthering Heights (St Ann's Warehouse/National/US Tour/Wise Children); Accidental Death of an Anarchist (Haymarket/Lyric/Sheffield); Cruise (Duchess); Scissors (Sheffield); August in England, House of Ife, Lava (Bush); Worth (Arcola/New Earth/Storyhouse); The Cherry Orchard (Yard/HOME); Cherry Jezebel (Liverpool Theatre); Birthmarked (Bristol Old Vic); I'll Take You To Mrs. Cole (Complicite); Big Big Sky, The Hoes (Hampstead); The Sorcerer's Apprentice (Northern Stage); Out of the Dark (Rose Theatre Kingston); Welcome Home, Shuck'n'Jive, Whitewash (Soho); Anansi the Spider (Unicorn); Glory (Duke's/Red Ladder); Cuzco (Theatre503); Losing Venice (Orange Tree); 46 Beacon (Trafalgar Studios with Rick Fisher); Out There on Fried Meat Ridge Road (White Bear/Trafalgar Studios 2); Acorn (Courtyard).**

Nick Powell (Sound Designer & Composer)

For the Royal Court: **The Glow, Living Newspaper, Bad Roads, The Ferryman (& West End/Broadway), X, Unreachable, The Mistress Contract, The Nether (& West End), The Ritual Slaughter of Gorge Mastromas, Talk Show, Narrative, Get Santa! [co-creator], The Vertical Hour, Relocated.**

Other theatre includes: **The Lehman Trilogy (West End/Broadway), The Glass Menagerie, The Mirror and the Light (West End); The Tell-Tale Heart, Othello (National); Julius Caesar (Bridge); Raya, Mary (Hampstead); Solar (Klangwolke, Linz); People, Places and Things (Stadsteatern, Stockholm); City of Glass (59 Productions); Alice in Wonderland (Lyceum, Edinburgh); Peter Pan, All My Sons, Lord of the Flies, The Crucible (Regent's Park Open Air/UK tour); Lanark: A Life in Three Acts (& Citizens, Glasgow), 27, The Wheel, The Wonderful World of Dissocia (& National Theatre of Scotland), Realism (Edinburgh International Festival); Dunsinane (& tour), A Life of Galileo, Richard**

III, The Drunks, God in Ruins (RSC); Urtain, Marat-Sade, Los Macbez (CDN, Madrid); Paradise (Rhurtriennale, Germany); 'Tis Pity She's a Whore (Cheek by Jowl); Penumbra, Tito Andronico (Animalario, Madrid); The Wolves in the Walls (& National Theatre of Scotland/New Victory, NYC/UK tour), Panic (Improbable); Wolf Hall/Bring Up the Bodies [as sound designer] (RSC/West End/Broadway).**

Exhibitions: **Frameless.**

Jonnie Riordan (Movement Director)

As movement director, for the Royal Court: **Hope has a Happy Meal.**

As movement director, other theatre includes: **The Book of Will (& Queen's Theatre Hornchurch/Shakespeare North), A Christmas Carol (Bolton Octagon); How Not to Drown (ThickSkin/Traverse); Great Apes (Arcola); Eyes closed, Ears covered (Bunker); Maggie and Pierre (Finborough), Mobile (The Paper Birds); Home (Frozen Light/UK Tour), Caught (Pleasance), A Tale of Two Cities (USF/Brit Project).**

As associate movement director, theatre includes: **Whisper House (Other Palace), Myth (RSC/Mischief Festival).**

As director, theatre includes: **Blood Harmony, Eavesdropping (& Traverse), PETRICHOR, AWOL (& Tron), Boy Magnet (& Theatr Clwyd) (ThickSkin); The Witchfinder's Sister (Queen's Theatre Hornchurch); Nigel Slater's Toast (West End/UK Tour).**

As associate director, theatre includes: **Things I Know to Be True (Frantic Assembly/UK Tour); The Static (& UK Tour), Blackout, Chalk Farm (& Bush/Off Broadway) (ThickSkin).**

Katie Stephen (Deputy Stage Manager)

As Deputy Stage Manager for the Royal Court: **Jews. In Their Own Words.**

As Assistant Stage Manager for the Royal Court: **Is God Is**

As Deputy Stage Manager, other theatre includes: **Private Lives (Donmar Warehouse), Jack & the Beanstalk (Crossroads Pantomimes, Bradford Alhambra), A Christmas Carol: On Air (Theatre Royal Windsor), Exodus (National Theatre of Scotland), Laurel & Hardy (Royal Lyceum Theatre Edinburgh), Sleeping Beauty (Crossroads Pantomimes, Bradford Alhambra)**

As Assistant Stage Manager, other theatre/opera includes: **The Fever Syndrome (Hampstead), The Life and Death of Alexander Litvinenko (Grange Park Opera), Ivan the Terrible (Grange Park Opera), Christmas Tales (Royal Lyceum**

Theatre), Goldilocks & the Three Bears (Qdos Pantomimes, King's Theatre Edinburgh), The Duchess [of Malfi] (Royal Lyceum Theatre Edinburgh)

As Stage Manager on the Book, theatre includes: **Svetlana (Ed Littlewood Productions), The Stornoway Way (Dogstar Theatre Company)**

Tom Turner
(Associate Lighting Designer)

As Associate Lighting Designer, theatre includes: **The Ocean at the End of the Lane (UK Tour); A Strange Loop (Barbican); Bat out of Hell The Musical (UK Tour); Matthew Bourne's Swan Lake (UK & International Tour); Les Misérables The Staged Concert (Gielgud); Elf (Dominion) and The Grinning Man (Trafalgar Studios).**

As Assistant Lighting Designer, theatre includes: **Chess (ENO); Bat out of Hell The Musical (Manchester & London).**

Selected Lighting Designs include: **In Clay (Vaults); 9 Circles (Park Theatre and Edinburgh Fringe); The Dog Walker (Jermyn Street), HGO's Venus/ Dido (Cockpit); HGO's La Traviata (Jackson's Lane and Teatro Modica); Red Bull Human Pinball (with Ammonite, Online).**

THE ROYAL COURT THEATRE

The Royal Court Theatre is the writers' theatre. It is a leading force in world theatre for cultivating and supporting writers – undiscovered, emerging and established.

Through the writers, the Royal Court is at the forefront of creating restless, alert, provocative theatre about now. We open our doors to the unheard voices and free thinkers that, through their writing, change our way of seeing.

Over 120,000 people visit the Royal Court in Sloane Square, London, each year and many thousands more see our work elsewhere through transfers to the West End and New York, UK and international tours, digital platforms, our residencies across London, and our site-specific work. Through all our work we strive to inspire audiences and influence future writers with radical thinking and provocative discussion.

The Royal Court's extensive development activity encompasses a diverse range of writers and artists and includes an ongoing programme of writers' attachments, readings, workshops and playwriting groups. Twenty years of the International Department's pioneering work around the world means the Royal Court has relationships with writers on every continent.

Since 1956 we have commissioned and produced hundreds of writers, from John Osborne to Jasmine Lee-Jones. Royal Court plays from every decade are now performed on stage and taught in classrooms and universities across the globe.

We strive to create an environment in which differing voices and opinions can co-exist. In current times, it is becoming increasingly difficult for writers to write what they want or need to write without fear, and we will do everything we can to rise above a narrowing of viewpoints.

It is because of this commitment to the writer and our future that we believe there is no more important theatre in the world than the Royal Court.

 royalcourt  royalcourttheatre

Supported using public funding by
ARTS COUNCIL ENGLAND

ROYAL

ASSISTED PERFORMANCES

Captioned Performances

Captioned performances are accessible for people who are D/deaf, deafened & hard of hearing, as well as being suitable for people for whom English is not a first language.

Hope has a Happy Meal
Friday 7th July 2023, 7:45pm

Cuckoo
Wednesday 2nd August 2023, 7:30pm
Thursday 3rd August 2023, 2:30pm
Saturday 12th August 2023, 2:30pm

Word-Play
Wednesday 16th August 2023, 7:45pm
Saturday 26th August 2023, 3pm

BSL-interpreted Performances

BSL-interpreted performances, delivered by an interpreter, give a sign inteprretation of the text spoken and/or sung by artists in the onstage production.

Cuckoo
Saturday 19th August 2023, 2:30pm

COURT

ROYAL

ASSISTED PERFORMANCES

Performances in a Relaxed Environment

Relaxed Environment performances are suitable for those who may benefit from a more relaxed environment.

During these performances:
- There is a relaxed attitude to noise in the auditorium; you are welcome to respond to the show in whatever way feels natural
- You can enter and exit the auditorium when needed
- We will help you find the best seats for your experience
- House lights may remain raised slightly
- Loud noises may be reduced

If you would like to talk to us about your access requirements, please contact our Box Office at (0)20 7565 5000 or boxoffice@royalcourttheatre.com

The Royal Court Visual Story is available on our website. Story and Sensory synposes are available on the show pages via the Whats On tab of the website shortly after Press Night.

COURT

ROYAL COURT SUPPORTERS

Our incredible community of supporters makes it possible for us to achieve our mission of nurturing and platforming writers at every stage of their careers. Our supporters are part of our essential fabric – they help to give us the freedom to take bigger and bolder risks in our work, develop and empower new voices, and create world-class theatre that challenges and disrupts the theatre ecology.

To all our supporters, thank you. You help us to write the future.

ROYAL

BAR & KITCHEN

The Royal Court's Bar & Kitchen aims to create a welcoming and inspiring environment with a style and ethos that reflects the work we put on stage.

Offering expertly crafted cocktails alongside an extensive selection of craft gins and beers, wine and soft drinks, our vibrant basement bar provides a sanctuary in the middle of Sloane Square. By day a perfect spot for meetings or quiet reflection and by night atmospheric meeting spaces for cast, crew, audiences and the general public.

All profits go directly to supporting the work of the Royal Court theatre, cultivating and supporting writers – undiscovered, emerging and established.

For more information, visit
royalcourttheatre.com/bar

HIRES & EVENTS

The Royal Court is available to hire for celebrations, rehearsals, meetings, filming, ceremonies and much more. Our two theatre spaces can be hired for conferences and showcases, and the building is a unique venue for bespoke events and receptions.

For more information, visit
royalcourttheatre.com/events

Sloane Square London, SW1W 8AS ⊖ Sloane Square ⇌ Victoria Station
🐦 royalcourt 🅕 theroyalcourttheatre 📷 royalcourttheatre

COURT

SUPPORT THE COURT AND BE A PART OF OUR FUTURE.

Our Friends and Good Friends are part of the fabric of the Royal Court. They are our regulars and together, we enjoy bold and restless theatre that provokes and challenges us all. Like all friends, they help us too. The income we receive from our memberships directly supports our mission, providing writers with the space and platform to experiment and develop their writing.

Become a Friend today and inspire the next generation of theatre makers.

Become a Friend (from £40 a year)

Benefits include:
- Priority Booking
- Advanced access to £12 Monday tickets for productions in the Jerwood Theatre Downstairs
- 10% discount in our Bar & Kitchen (including Court in the Square) and Samuel French bookshop

Become a Good Friend (from £95 a year)

Our Good Friends' membership also includes a voluntary donation. This extra support goes directly towards supporting our work and future, both on and off stage.

In addition to the Friend benefits, our Good Friends also receive:

- Five complimentary playtexts for Royal Court productions
- An invitation for two to step behind the scenes of the Rpyal Court Theatre at a special annual event

To become a Friend or a Good Friend, or to find out more about the different ways in which you can get involved, visit our website: royalcourttheatre.com/support-us

The English Stage Company at the Royal Court Theatre is a registered charity (No. 231242)

LIVERPOOL
everyman
&PLAYHOUSE

At the Liverpool Everyman & Playhouse, we believe that theatre inspires creative lives. We bring artists, audiences and our communities together in a celebration of what great theatre can achieve.

With two exceptional Liverpool venues united by our mission to entertain and inspire, we create unforgettable experiences built from innovation, talent and a passion for social change.

Whether you visit us at the Everyman or the Playhouse, enjoy a co-production at a partner theatre, see our work online, or out in the community, we promise you an exhilarating theatrical adventure and a whole new way of looking at the world.

We're grateful for the continued support of Arts Council England, Liverpool City Council, our donors, patrons, partners and our audiences.

Find out more at **everymanplayhouse.com**

Chief Executive **Mark Da Vanzo**   Creative Director **Suba Das**

Trustees **Andrea Nixon** (Chair), **Paul Bibby**, **James Bierman**, **Helen Blakeman**, **Natasha Bucknor**, **Amy Causley**, **Mike Clarke**, **Paul Evans**, **Jill Jones**, **Camilla Mankabady**, **Caroline Sanger-Davies** and **Tony Smith**

Thank you to all Liverpool Everyman & Playhouse Staff

/everymanplayhouse
@LivEveryPlay
@LivEveryPlay

Cuckoo

Michael Wynne was born and brought up in Birkenhead. His first play, *The Knocky* (Meyer-Whitworth Award – Best New Playwright and Best New Writer Nomination – Writers' Guild), was produced by the Royal Court. His other credits for the Royal Court include *Who Cares*, *The Priory* (Olivier Award – Best New Comedy), *The People Are Friendly*, *The Red Flag*, *Friday Night Sex* (with Alecky Blythe) and *I'm Not Here – The Living Newspaper*. Wynne's work also includes the first new play at the rebuilt Liverpool Everyman, *Hope Place*, and *Canvas* (Minerva Theatre, Chichester), *Sell Out* (Best Off West End – Time Out Theatre Awards) and *Dirty Wonderland* (both Frantic Assembly), *Tits/Teeth* (Soho Theatre), *The Boy Who Left Home* (Actors Touring Company), *We Are Here* (La Mama, New York) and *The Star* (Liverpool Playhouse). He has also written extensively for screen, including *My Summer of Love* (BAFTA – Best British Film, Evening Standard Film Awards; Best Screenplay, the Michael Powell Award for Best British Film at the Edinburgh Film Festival; joint winner of the Directors' Guild Award for Best British Film), *Lapland* and *Being Eileen* for the BBC.

MICHAEL WYNNE

Cuckoo

faber

First published in 2023
by Faber and Faber Limited
The Bindery, 51 Hatton Garden
London, EC1N 8HN

Typeset by Brighton Gray
Printed and bound in the UK by CPI Group (Ltd), Croydon CR0 4YY

A CIP record for this book
is available from the British Library

ISBN 978-0-571-38610-9

Printed and bound in the UK on FSC® certified paper in line with our continuing
commitment to ethical business practices, sustainability and the environment.
For further information see faber.co.uk/environmental-policy

2 4 6 8 10 9 7 5 3 1

Acknowledgements

I would like to say a huge thank you to Vicky Featherstone, Dominic Cooke, Debra Oswald, Rachel Kavanaugh, Lucy Morrison, Jane Fallowfield, Sean O'Connor, Robin Hooper, Graham Clayton-Chance, Fiona Sutton and Margaret Anne Dunne.

I also couldn't do any of this without the never-ending support of Michael McCoy and my wonderful mum and sisters.

Cuckoo was first performed at the Royal Court Jerwood Theatre Downstairs, London, on 6 July 2023, with the following cast:

Carmel Michelle Butterly
Megyn Emma Harrison
Doreen Sue Jenkins
Sarah Jodie McNee

Director Vicky Featherstone
Designer Peter McKintosh
Lighting Designer Jai Morjaria
Sound Designer and Composer Nick Powell
Movement Director Jonnie Riordan
Assistant Director Jade Franks
Associate Lighting Designer Tom Turner
Deputy Stage Manager Katie Stephen
Assistant Stage Manager Lottie Denby
Sound Operator Florence Hand
Set built by Ridiculous Solutions

For Paul Keating

Characters

Doreen

Carmel
Doreen's daughter

Sarah
Doreen's daughter

Megyn
Carmel's seventeen-year-old daughter

CUCKOO

Note

Phone pings and alerts make different sounds
depending on what they are.

Act One

Doreen's house.

Birkenhead.

Dining room.

Evening.

A round dining table and chairs in the centre.

A sideboard with framed family photos, nick-nacks and a couple of small potted plants.

Colourful curtains are closed in front of patio doors – which lead to a small garden.

The kitchen – which we can't see – is through a door to the left, which leads through to the hallway and stairs to the upstairs.

It's an early spring evening.

Three women are sat round the table – all looking at their mobile phones in silence.

Doreen, her daughter Carmel, and Megyn, Carmel's seventeen-year-old daughter.

Megyn looks younger than seventeen.

Carmel scrolls through her phone.

Doreen is busy reading.

Megyn is similarly engrossed – with lots of two-hand typing.

They sit in silence. And don't look up. For a long time.
Longer than feels comfortable.

Carmel's phone pings. She looks at the message, laughs to herself and replies.

Pause. Silence.

Doreen's phone pings, with a different sound. She reads the message, thinks and replies.

Pause. Silence.

Megyn's phone pings, with another sound. She doesn't look up and reads.

Doreen's phone pings.

Doreen She's on her way back.

Doreen texts a reply and goes off into the kitchen. Leaving her phone on the table.
Carmel and Megyn don't look up from their phones.
Carmel's phone plays a snippet of the Benny Hill *theme tune – she watches it for a second and smiles. Then swipes it away.*
Megyn doesn't look up.
Long pause.
Doreen's phone makes the sound of a cash register. She comes through with knives and forks and salt and vinegar. She puts them in the middle of the table and looks at her phone.

Just sold that cardigan. That's good.

She sits down and types a response.
Carmel's phone pings. She laughs. She forwards the text.

Carmel (*to Doreen*) I just sent you something funny. The stuff Kerry sends me, cracks me up.

Doreen's phone pings. Doreen looks at her phone. She laughs.

Doreen That's funny that. Oh I like that.

She laughs some more.

Carmel Isn't it great.

Doreen I'll have to send that to Pat McMahon. She'll love that. (*To Megyn.*) I've just sent it to you. Make you smile.

Carmel You won't get a smile out of her.

Megyn's phone pings. She doesn't look up. She looks at her phone and smiles. She types a response to Doreen.
Doreen receives it with a ping.

Doreen (*to Megyn*) Yeah, I know. That's just what I thought.

Doreen chuckles to herself.
   They all look at their phones in silence.
   Another pause.
   Megyn's phone pings. She replies.
   Carmel's phone pings in quick succession. She reads.

Carmel You can get lost.

She types a response.
   Sarah enters through the back door in the kitchen, off.

Sarah (*off*) I'm back.

*She comes into the room with two – of her own – tote
bags. One full of wrapped portions of fish and chips and
another with four canned drinks.*

Here we go.

Doreen I've put the plates in the oven.

Doreen goes off to get the plates.
   *Sarah takes the fish and chips out of the bag at the
table – they're all wrapped up in paper.*
   *Doreen brings the plates from the oven with a tea towel
and puts them out on the table.*

Don't touch the plates! They're hot.

Doreen goes back into the kitchen.
   *Sarah hands the parcels out. They each open the parcels
and prepare to eat the food out of the paper on the plates.*

Sarah One for you.

Carmel Ta, hun.

Sarah And curry sauce there for y'.

She takes out a small pot of curry sauce.

Carmel This is just what I need.

Sarah He put a cross on one. Just chips and no vinegar. For
Megyn.

She passes Megyn the parcel with the cross on.

Megyn (*quiet*) Ta.

Sarah You sure you don't want some fish?

Megyn shakes her head.
Doreen brings in a few rounds of buttered white bread on a plate.

Doreen Bread and butter there.

Sarah places a fish and chips on Doreen's plate and one on hers.

Sarah Mum.

Doreen Thanks, love.

Sarah goes off into the kitchen.
Carmel's phone pings. She looks at it and texts a reply.

I'm not gonna eat all that. Look at all these chips. Is this a regular portion? I didn't want a big one. I wanted a regular portion.

Sarah (*off*) It's a regular portion.

Doreen I should have got one of those small senior citizens ones.

Sarah comes back with four glasses and dishes out the drinks.

Sarah Coke, Diet Coke, Seven Up, Tango.

Doreen Ta.

Doreen and Sarah pour their drinks into the glass. Carmel and Megyn drink from the cans.
They all start tucking into their food.
Megyn picks at her food and doesn't eat much.
Carmel and Megyn pick up their phones, and look at them as they eat.

Did you go to the one down the bottom?

Sarah Yeah. The one across there has gone right downhill. I don't know who's running it now. Stunk of disinfectant last time I went.

Doreen Too handy with their bleach. Think they can throw some bleach around and the place is clean.

They all eat.
  Carmel and Megyn are on their phones.
  Doreen's phone pings. She picks it up, reads and responds. She carries on looking at her phone.
  Sarah takes her phone out and looks at it too.
  They eat and all look at their phones.
  Long pause.
  Sarah looks up and sees that they're all looking at their phones.

Sarah Are we all just gonna sit on our phones?

Carmel Er, yeah.

Sarah Have we got nothing to say to each other?

Carmel I haven't, no.

Her phone pings. She looks at it. Then she carries on with what she was saying.

But if you've got something scintillating to say, fire away.

Sarah Shall we just put them down for a minute?

She puts hers away in her pocket.

Doreen Of course. Yeah.

Doreen closes the cover on hers and puts it away.
  Carmel puts hers on the table face up.
  Megyn puts her phone on her lap. She still texts and looks at it surreptitiously under the table.
  They all eat in silence.
  Pause.

Sarah (*about the food*) It's nice this isn't it.

Doreen Oh yeah.

Carmel Hmmm.

Sarah looks to Megyn. Megyn smiles back at her – she's enjoying it too.
Carmel pours some curry sauce onto her chips.

Doreen Much better than across there.

Sarah You can't beat a chippy tea. Fish and chips.

Doreen You can't.

Pause.

Sarah We had to exclude two more pupils today. One brought in a meat cleaver. The other for cupping the balls of another boy, again. Both six.

Carmel Little bastards.

Sarah And if it's not the kids it's the parents. We had two dads scrapping in the playground yesterday. We managed to split them up. But then one of them went to his car and came back with a crossbow. Had this other dad up against the caretaker's Nissan. We had to call the police. This is all before nine a.m. in a primary school.

They all eat.

Oh, I've ordered flowers off Kevin.

Doreen looks at Sarah, she's not sure what she means.

For Saturday. For me dad.

Doreen Of course.

Sarah I can't believe it's another year already.

Doreen Hmmm I know.

Sarah I got red roses. We liked them last time. I can take us all up the cemetery on Saturday morning. Yeah?

Carmel Yeah.

Doreen Yeah.

Sarah looks towards Megyn.

Carmel *She* won't come. She still doesn't like cemeteries.

Sarah Did I tell you I bumped into Ronnie Boyle last week? I was in the little Tesco's on Borough Road, getting some tomato soup. (*To Doreen.*) He was asking how you were. I said you were okay. Getting on with your life. That the house is still quiet blah blah blah . . . And he just burst out crying. Then I was crying. Oh God it was . . .

Carmel I've seen him a couple of times since and as soon as he sees me, he's in bits.

Sarah He just loved me dad didn't he. They go right back. Six-foot bricklayer who you'd think had never cried in his life. And there he is, sobbing by the soup.

Carmel It's a bit much though isn't it. I ended up having to comfort him in the middle of Grange Road West. And it's not like it only happened yesterday. It's years now.

Doreen I saw him and Jill the other week in Superdrug and . . .

Carmel What have I told you about going in Superdrug? If everyone goes in Superdrug then that's me out of a job in Boots isn't it.

Doreen I'm sorry. It was raining and I just needed some dental floss and Superdrug was there right in front of me.

Carmel We're literally next door.

Doreen Anyway, I saw them and knew Ronnie'd be crying if he saw me, so I hid down by the cotton buds.

Sarah You didn't?

Doreen I just couldn't be doing with it.

Sarah You shouldn't do that.

Carmel She can do whatever she wants. Me mum doesn't need him upsetting her.

Sarah Oh, I know, but . . .

Carmel casually makes herself a chip butty.
Pause.

Doreen This fish *is* nice. Though I'm not gonna be able to eat all of it.

Sarah Me dad never liked fish and chips, did he?

Carmel Ooh no.

Sarah What was it, the smell or . . .?

Doreen You know he could be fussy about some things.

Megyn's phone pings. She subtly looks at it in her lap.

Carmel Ah Megyn, you should have that on silent. (*To Sarah.*) What's the punishment for a pinging phone?

Sarah Don't be daft.

Pause.

Eh, I'm still seeing that bloke I like.

Doreen The dishy dentist?

Sarah Yeah, Simon. I think he's a keeper.

Doreen Has he got lovely teeth? Dentists always have lovely teeth.

Sarah They are nice, yeah.

Doreen He must be clever to be a dentist. Maybe not doctor clever but he'd still have to be bright.

Sarah He is. The stuff he comes out with. He knows everything.

Doreen You haven't mentioned him very much.

Sarah I didn't know how it would go, but now, I think . . . It looks like he's going to stick around. He's not from round here, just moved up here from down south. Temporarily at first.

Doreen There's a lot of clever people down south.

Carmel Yeah, we're all thick up here, aren't we?

Doreen I didn't mean it like that.

Sarah The last few weeks we've been messaging each other all day long. Like a couple of teenagers. He's handsome too. I've got some nice pictures now.

Sarah takes her phone out and looks through her photos.

Carmel So, you're allowed to get your phone out?

Sarah It's fine . . . (*She looks through photos on her phone.*) Not that one. His chin looks a bit weird there. There's a better one. Oh, ee are . . .

Sarah shows her phone to Doreen.

Doreen Ooh yeah.

Sarah finds another photo.

Sarah I like this one.

Doreen All in blue.

Sarah Brings out his eyes.

Doreen Any of his teeth? You can't see his teeth in these.

Sarah looks on her phone.

Sarah I don't think so.

Doreen You'd think if you were a dentist and had lovely teeth, you'd be showing them off all day long. Like advertising for your business.

Sarah gives up looking.

Sarah He's so thoughtful. Just sends me texts out of the blue. 'Thinking about you.'

Her phone pings.

Oh my God. That's him now. How weird is that?

Carmel Really weird.

Sarah (*reading*) 'How's your fish and chips?' I told him we were having fish and chips. It's like he appeared because I mentioned him. Conjured him up.

Doreen Ah yeah.

Sarah (*texting back*) 'Nice thanks. I was just talking about you. How funny.' I mean, I just . . . I feel he's . . . I don't wanna jinx it by going on about him . . .

Carmel Yeah, best not.

Doreen As long as you're happy. What happened to that ginger farmer? I liked the sound of him.

Sarah It didn't work out. It's fine. I met Simon on here. (*Pointing to her phone.*) There's no shame in online dating any more.

Doreen Even dentists?

Sarah Everyone's on here. (*To Megyn.*) You should have a look. Find yourself a nice boyfriend.

Carmel Her? Don't make me laugh. Who'd be interested in her?

Doreen Carmel.

Sarah (*to Carmel*) Or you.

Carmel I'm done with men.

Sarah You're into women now, are you?

Doreen Sarah.

Carmel Of course, I'm not.

Megyn There's nothing wrong with being a lesbian.

Carmel Oh, it speaks!

Doreen We don't need that sort of talk when I'm eating me fish . . .

Carmel And nobody said there was anything wrong with being a . . . y' know . . .

Megyn Lesbian.

Doreen Megyn, please.

Short pause. They eat.
Megyn looks at her phone. Doreen gets a ping.

(*To Sarah.*) Can I just look at this?

Sarah Of course.

Doreen reads the message and replies.
They eat. Pause.
Carmel's phone pings. She looks at it on the table but doesn't pick it up.
She leisurely makes herself another chip butty.
Doreen's phone makes a news flash alert sound. She looks at it.

Doreen It's a news flash!

Sarah What's happened?

Carmel It'll be something bad if it's a news flash.

Doreen (*reading*) 'A van has driven into a crowded market square in Germany injuring many.'

Sarah Oh God.

Carmel's phone makes a different news flash sound. She picks it up.

Carmel Oh, ee are. (*Reading.*) 'Heidelberg Market Square Major Incident.'

Doreen It's meant to be nice, Heidelberg. I think your dad went there once.

Sarah Why haven't I had a news flash? (*To Megyn.*) Have you got a news flash?

Megyn's phone makes a news flash sound. She takes her phone out from on her lap and looks at it.

Now you've got one. I want news flashes too.

Carmel, Doreen and Megyn are all on their phones.

Megyn Three dead.

Doreen Have you got them turned off?

Sarah I didn't think so. Let me see.

She checks the settings on her phone.

Carmel I thought you weren't interested in phones?

Sarah I'd like to know if something happens.

Megyn 'Driver shot dead by police.'

Sarah I've got them turned off for some reason. I'll turn it back on.

Doreen It says here they don't know if it's an accident or terrorist attack yet.

Sarah It could be an accident. Fell asleep at the wheel or . . .

Carmel That's no accident. All you need is a driver's licence to be a terrorist these days.

Megyn 'Loud bang in another part of the city.'

Doreen Oh, my goodness.

Sarah It must be terrifying.

Megyn 'Police think there might be other attacks.'

Carmel There's a video here.

Sarah Let's have a look.

She holds her phone out in front of her horizontally on the table so they can all see. They move in close.

Carmel It says there's no sound.

Sarah Do I wanna see this?

Carmel You don't have to watch.

Carmel presses play. They all watch in silence. Pause.

Doreen I don't know what I'm looking at. Oh, I see. It is pretty, Heidelberg.

Carmel There's the van. In white.

Sarah He's all over the place.

Doreen Oh goodness.

Sarah Oh oh . . .

Carmel Just missed that bloke.

Doreen It's gone right into those people.

The video has stopped.

Carmel Is that it? You could hardly see anything.

Carmel turns the phone back to vertical and goes back to looking at it just herself.
They all continue looking at their phones.

Sarah People don't run when something bad happens these days, they start filming.

Megyn Five dead now.

Doreen Poor people.

Sarah, Doreen and Carmel put their phones on the table.
Megyn puts hers back in her lap.
Pause.

Sarah (*to Megyn*) While I remember, our new head, Felicity, she's brilliant, said you could come in and do some work experience. Follow me round, see if you like it.

They all look to her.
Megyn doesn't say anything.

Doreen That's good isn't it, Megyn?

27

Sarah What d'you think?

Carmel What do you say to getting out the house? Was half a battle to get her to come here.

Doreen She likes coming here. You like coming here, don't you?

Megyn doesn't answer.

Sarah One of the perks is the school being across the road from your nan's, you can pop in here on your dinner break.

They all look to Megyn again.

And you get to hang out with your Auntie Sarah. What d'you think?

Megyn (*quiet, inaudible*) I'm not sure.

Sarah What did you say? What did she say?

Carmel She might be better texting you.

Doreen Stop it you.

Megyn (*quiet, to Sarah*) Can I think about it? I'm not sure . . .

Carmel Have you got some other job offers in? Other irons in the fire? Need to weigh up all the different options?

Sarah (*to Carmel*) That's enough.

Megyn (*forceful, to Carmel*) I just wanna think about it, okay?

Carmel Oooh. Okay, okay.

Sarah No pressure. Of course. You think about it.

Carmel Yeah, you let us know.

Pause.

Doreen I'm really struggling with this fish.

Sarah I think you'd enjoy it and Felicity is lovely. You'll love her.

Carmel While I remember. Got a load of samples from work they were gonna throw out.

She takes out a plastic Boots bag with lots of samples inside.

The shampoo and moisturisers are good. The body cream smells like a cat's sprayed, I'd steer clear.

Sarah Felicity's got so many brilliant ideas and she's political. She thinks schools, education . . . What we do, is political. Especially state schools. If it was up to her, she'd close down all private schools. Says all kids should mix together from day dot.

Doreen takes some samples out of the bag.

Doreen I do love a sample. (*She reads one of the labels.*) Juniper and mimosa. Oooh.

Sarah She's really shaking up the teaching staff. Has us playing all these games and doing exercises. Like proper exercises. Boot camp the other day.

Doreen (*sniffing another sample*) Minty one, nice.

Sarah She had us all running round the playground before the kids came in. I nearly threw up but I felt great afterwards . . .

Doreen passes the bag to Sarah.

I'll look when I've finished me . . .

She points to her food. Doreen passes the bag to Megyn.

Carmel She won't be interested. You're not, are y'?

Megyn shakes her head.
Doreen passes the bag back to Carmel.

Sarah She wants to make some big changes, Felicity. She's really into the environment, wants us to become an official green school.

Doreen That's nice. Are you going to have a few more trees round the playground?

Megyn smirks. Carmel gives her a sharp look.

Sarah Well yeah, but it's a bit more than that. Get solar panels so we generate our own power, grow vegetables for the dinners, become plastic free, car free blah blah blah . . .

Doreen Oh right.

Sarah It'd be brilliant to grow our own food and get the kids involved in that. I'm all for that but some of it is going to be really hard. A plastic-free school? Virtually everything in a primary school is plastic. Cups, pens, toys. The laminator. My favourite thing in the school. I love laminating things. It brings me so much pleasure. That has to go.

Carmel And no cars?

Sarah We're going to put greenhouses on the car park. I'm gonna have to get a bike . . .

Carmel You hate cycling. Ever since you went over the handlebars outside here and smashed your front teeth.

Sarah That was ages ago. I'm sure I'll love it. It'll get me fit. She might have a bit of a fight on her hands, banning all cars, apart from electric ones. Not all of the staff live nearby. Virtually all the kids can walk in though.

Carmel I bet she doesn't have to come far.

Sarah No, she lives up the top in Oxton Village. She's got a bike. And an electric car.

Carmel Of course she has.

Doreen I wouldn't want to be getting on a bike in the winter. I'm sure she'll let you drive in if it's wet.

Sarah It's about more than the weather, Mum.

Carmel I'm not giving up my car for anything. It's a piece of shit but it gets me around.

Doreen You can't rely on the buses round here any more. They're terrible.

Carmel I know.

Doreen They change the timetable overnight or they often just don't turn up. We don't have any in the evening or weekend now. And there's no one to complain to. When we first moved here there were no cars in this street. Only your dad and Tall Brian on the end. The buses ran like clockwork. Now the street's full of cars and there's nowhere to park. Them opposite have got four cars. Him and her have got one each and now the daughters too. It's ridiculous.

Sarah We'll all have to get rid of our cars in the future.

Megyn We will. We'll have to use bikes.

Carmel (*to Megyn*) I'd like to see you get on a bike if we had no car.

Doreen I think I'm a bit old to be jumping on a pushbike.

Sarah Or more and better buses.

Doreen I'm all for that.

Sarah Felicity did this assembly for the whole school the other day about what's really going on, with the environment. Lots of stuff you know but when she put it all together . . . The seas full of plastic, the burning rainforests, melting ice caps, whole species dying out, crazy weather . . . All coming together at once. It was shocking . . . Some of the little kids were upset, frightened . . .

Carmel That's nice.

Sarah It was a bit much . . .

Megyn It's just the truth and they need to know.

Carmel Who rattled your cage?

Sarah I think she's a breath of fresh air. She's more hardcore than me, into demonstrations and disruption to get politicians to act. She's even into kids going on strike, bunking off school, which is an odd position for a headteacher . . .

Carmel She sounds like a friggin' loony.

Megyn I like the sound of her.

Sarah Even more reason for you to come and work in the school. You'll love each other.

Doreen Who's gonna help me with this fish?

Carmel For fuck's sake. Go 'head then.

    Doreen cuts her fish in half and puts it on Carmel's plate.

Doreen And what about some of these chips?

Carmel Mother, just leave them if you don't want them all.

    Pause.

Doreen I try not to use plastic bags any more.

    Megyn half scoffs to herself.

Carmel Are you finding something funny?

Megyn No.

Carmel What are you laughing at then?

Megyn This is about more than plastic bags.

Doreen And I try and recycle where I can.

Carmel Don't have a go at your nan for doing her bit.

Megyn I wasn't but this is an emergency.

Sarah I do think we'll need to make dramatic changes to the way we live. But if we all do small things, we can make a difference.

Megyn If we don't act now the world is going to end.

Carmel Oh Christ.

Doreen I thought I was . . .

Megyn You've got to take it seriously.

Doreen Oh, okay.

Sarah She's right.

Carmel I've got bigger things to think about.

Megyn Bigger than the end of the planet?

Carmel I haven't got the luxury like Felicity, in her electric car, to cry about the ice caps melting . . .

Megyn It's not a luxury.

Carmel It is for me when I've got a mortgage and bills to pay to make sure you're fed and there's a roof over your head. Especially this last year since they made me part time at work out of the blue. If you wanna take on those responsibilities while I go and paint meself red and lie in the road, then great.

Megyn I can't say anything.

Carmel You happy to swap roles? Are you, eh?

Doreen Leave it now.

Megyn You don't understand.

Sarah It's good that she's speaking up, feels strongly about . . .

Carmel But she doesn't know what she's talking about.

Megyn I do.

Carmel She can get on her high horse because she has nothing real to worry about . . .

Doreen That's enough.

Pause.

I do love some David Attenborough, but even he can be a bit of a miz bag now, always going on about climate change . . . You don't want to think about the end of the world before you go to bed on a Sunday night.

33

Sarah I hate that you'll be watching these cute seals playing about in the water and the next minute some huge shark appears and eats them all. Pretty little bunnies frolicking about, aw, pack of wolves turn up and rips them to pieces . . .

Megyn starts crying.
Pause.

Carmel Here we go.

Sarah Ah, Megyn . . .

Doreen There's no need to get upset.

Sarah Is this about David Attenborough?

Carmel I get this all the time.

Megyn Stop it, stop it, stop it.

Megyn cries more.
Pause.

Doreen Megyn, you okay?

Carmel We getting the full firework display?

Sarah Carmel! Megyn, it's okay . . .

Sarah reaches out to Megyn but she flinches.

Oh Megyn. I was only . . .

Doreen What's wrong?

Megyn It's . . . It's . . .

They all look at her.

Sarah Go on.

She shakes her head and runs out the room, through the kitchen and upstairs. We hear her going up the stairs and a door slams.

Carmel For crying out loud.

Doreen What's that all about?

Carmel This is what she does.

Sarah She's like this?

Carmel Or variations on a theme.

Doreen You are hard on her.

Carmel I'm no harder than I am on anyone else.

Sarah You're relentless sometimes.

Carmel (*to Sarah*) It was your fault talking about Armageddon.

Sarah That's not what I was saying.

Doreen Has she got upset about this before?

Carmel She gets upset if you don't agree with her.

Doreen She is very sensitive.

Carmel She needs to toughen up.

Doreen She can be very quiet. Hardly speaks sometimes.

Sarah She just seems so sad. It breaks your heart. She used to be so happy.

Carmel Here she goes. Don't make it into a bigger drama than it is. Megyn's all mouth on here – (*Pointing to her phone.*) firing off grand opinions, but if you disagree with her in the real world she can't cope.

Doreen Since she left school, she's been more . . .

Sarah Is she going after any jobs?

Carmel God no. What could she do?

Sarah There's loads of things.

Carmel She left school with no qualifications and she's got no interest in anything.

Sarah I'll get her into the school, that'll be a start.

Carmel She won't do that.

Sarah She might.

Carmel She won't.

Sarah D'you think she's got worse since . . .?

Carmel That's got nothing to do with it.

Doreen Do you wanna go and see she's okay?

Carmel She'll be down in a minute and we'll all just pretend nothing happened.

Carmel scrolls through her phone.
Pause.

Doreen I haven't got anything for afters.

Carmel I should have got some choc ices.

They've all finished eating. Sarah eats one last chip then pushes her plate away.

Sarah I couldn't eat another thing.

Awkward pause.
Doreen and Sarah look up above them towards where Megyn is.

I think you should go and see she's alright.

Carmel For Christ's sake. (*Not getting up, shouting upstairs.*) Megyn, you okay? Come down now.

Sarah Oh, the compassion.

Carmel I'm the one who has to live with her. You don't know the half of it. She can be a right little madam.

Doreen Should I . . .?

Carmel Leave her.

Sarah Let me go and talk to her. I'm good with her.

Carmel Are you now?

Sarah We've always had a special little bond, her Auntie Sarah.

Carmel If you say so.

Sarah goes out through the kitchen and upstairs.

Don't go making it worse.

We hear her footsteps going up the stairs.
Doreen and Carmel are left alone. Carmel looks at her phone.

Doreen I thought I was doing a good thing not using plastic bags. And it's a right pain sometimes.

Carmel You are. It's fine.

Doreen's phone rings. Her ringtone is 'Single Ladies' by Beyoncé.
She looks at it – she's flustered.

Doreen Ooh I've got to take this.

She makes her way through to the kitchen.

Carmel You can talk in here, I don't mind.

Doreen *(off)* Hello?

Then just the muffled sound of her talking on the phone.
Carmel listens out for Sarah upstairs but can't hear anything.
She scrolls through her phone.
Doreen lets out a shriek of laughter from the kitchen.
Carmel turns and looks towards the kitchen, surprised.

Doreen *(off)* Don't be silly.

And another long laugh.

Carmel *(to herself)* Who the hell is that?

Doreen *(off)* Oh stop it. Shush.

Carmel gets up and moves towards the kitchen doorway.
She listens.

37

(*Off, giggling.*) Oh stop it . . . No, you put the phone down first . . . No, you . . . (*She laughs some more.*) Oh you have. Oh . . .

> *Carmel sits back down quickly and looks at her phone.*
> *Doreen comes back in. She puts her phone on the table.*

Are we all done here?

Carmel God yeah.

> *Doreen clears the plates and paper away. She looks at Megyn's plate.*

Doreen She's hardly touched any of this.

> *She clears the rest of the plates.*

Carmel Who was that?

Doreen You what?

Carmel The phone? On the phone?

Doreen Oh that. Just about something I'm selling online. Mix-up. Thing.

Carmel Right.

Doreen Yeah.

Carmel They were really making you laugh.

Doreen Oh yeah. He's funny. Was funny. Very funny.

Carmel Hmmm yeah.

> *Doreen takes the plates into the kitchen.*
> *Carmel goes back to the security of her phone.*
> *She looks at something which plays Frank Sinatra singing 'I did it my way . . . ' She watches and smiles. Then swipes to something else.*

(*Shouting through.*) What d'you reckon to this?

> *Doreen comes in. Carmel shows the screen to Doreen.*

Doreen Isn't that funny. I've been watching a red one of those for ages.

Carmel Brand new with tags.

Doreen Ooh yeah. You gonna get it?

Doreen takes the salt and vinegar, glasses and empty cans through to the kitchen.

Carmel I'll just keep an eye on it for now.

She scrolls through her phone. We hear a snippet of 'I Like to Move It'. She quickly scrolls to something else.
Carmel looks up above her to where Megyn and Sarah are.
Doreen comes back in and sits down. She looks at her phone.

Doreen Aw look at Lewis. Pat Smith's grandson. He's the fattest cutest baby I've ever seen.

Doreen shows Carmel the picture on her phone.

Carmel Face like a football.

Carmel's phone pings. She looks at it.

As if?

She texts a reply.
Footsteps can be heard coming down the stairs. Carmel listens out.
Sarah comes through the kitchen and into the dining room.

No luck then?

Doreen Where is she?

Sarah She's . . .

Doreen Is she okay?

Sarah I don't know how to say this.

Carmel Spit it out.

Sarah (*to Doreen*) She's in your bed.

Carmel You what?

Doreen And what's she doing in there?

Sarah She said she's staying here.

Carmel What the hell did you say to her?

Sarah I just asked her if she was alright and . . .

Carmel I knew you'd make it worse. You always do. I've had enough of this.

She gets up to go and get her.

Sarah Hang on a mo. Listen to what she said . . .

They look at Sarah. She pauses – almost for dramatic effect.

Carmel Go on then.

Sarah She said . . . she's scared.

Carmel What?

Sarah She's frightened.

Doreen What of?

Sarah She wouldn't say.

Doreen What's there to be scared of?

Sarah I asked her. It's like she didn't know.

Carmel What the . . .? You were up there all of five minutes. Is it this environment nonsense?

Sarah I asked if it was that. She didn't say it was.

Doreen Has something happened to her?

Carmel Chance'd be a fine thing. She never leaves the house.

Doreen Is she too scared to come back down?

Carmel I'll give her something to be scared of.

Sarah She just said she feels safe here.

Doreen Aah. Has someone done something to her? Said something?

Sarah She wouldn't say.

Doreen That's really unsettled me, that . . .

Carmel You're all getting carried away.

Doreen The thought of her up there all frightened. I'll go and . . .

Carmel No. This'll be one of her games. She just wants the attention.

She goes through to the kitchen and shouts up.

(*Off.*) Are you coming down or what?

Doreen Carmel.

Carmel (*off*) Get out of me mother's bed and come down here now.

Carmel comes back through.

This is what I have to put up with.

Sarah (*sarcastic*) I think you handled that really well. (*She mock listens.*) Is that the pitter-patter of tiny feet coming down the stairs I can hear? No.

Carmel Oh, sod off.

Doreen Now . . .

Carmel You don't know what it's like. (*She takes her phone out.*) There's only one way to communicate with her . . .

She texts a message. She reads it out as she types it.

'I'm going home now. If you are coming, then come now.'

She presses send.
  A faint ping can be heard from upstairs. They all look upstairs above them.
  Carmel looks at her phone.

Oh. She's typing a reply.

They all look at the phone. Pause.

A love heart.

Doreen Aah.

Sarah That's nice.

Carmel (*shouting up above her*) I'll give you a friggin' love heart.

Doreen She can stay tonight if she wants.

Sarah Where will you sleep? Our old rooms are full of junk, aren't they?

Doreen I'll find somewhere. The sofa's . . .

Carmel I'm not having me mother sleeping on a sofa while she's . . .

Doreen It's fine.

Carmel I'm going.

Sarah (*to Carmel*) You gonna go?

Carmel Yeah, if she wants to play silly beggars . . . Come on.

Doreen gets her purse and takes out a ten-pound note.

Doreen (*to Sarah*) That's towards the fish and chips.

Sarah You don't need to do that.

Doreen Take it. I've just sold that cardigan.

Sarah Yours wasn't that much.

Doreen Take it.

Sarah takes the money.

Carmel (*to Sarah*) Can I give some towards it another . . .

Sarah It's fine. (*To Doreen.*) You gonna be okay, Mum?

Doreen Of course.

Sarah heads out through the kitchen.

Sarah T'ra, Mum.

They leave.

Carmel Just call me if she . . . T'ra.

Carmel heads off into the kitchen.

(*Off, shouting upstairs.*) I'm going!

Doreen follows them off into the kitchen.

Doreen (*off*) T'ra. T'ra now.

We hear the back door being closed and locked.
    Doreen comes back into the dining room and sits at the table. She looks up above her, towards the room Megyn is in.
    She takes out her phone, types out a text and sends it.
    She listens out and hears a faint ping from the upstairs room. She sits and waits.
    Pause.
    She looks at her phone. It pings. She reads the message and replies.
    Another faint ping in the distance.
    Pause.
    Then another ping on Doreen's phone.
    Lights fade as she types another message.
    End of Act One.

Act Two

Dining room as before.
  Three weeks later.
  Afternoon.
  It's raining heavily outside.
  The curtains are now open and we can see the closed patio doors. There's a small garden outside with many potted plants.
  Doreen is at the table packing up ornaments, clothes and other oddities that she's selling online.
  She has a small production line with items to be wrapped in one pile on the table and already wrapped and labelled items in another pile on the sideboard. There's old cardboard boxes, bubble wrap and a large tape dispenser on a handle for wrapping. It's very organised.
  She wraps an ornament in bubble wrap, places it in a cardboard box and tapes it shut.
  She checks the address on her iPad – which is on a little stand – then writes the address on the front with a marker. She then places it on the sideboard with other wrapped parcels.
  A real sense of satisfaction when she's wrapped an item.
  She takes a scarf from her pile of items to wrap and starts to package it.
  There's an iron and ironing board all set up next to the dining table.
  Carmel arrives in the kitchen.

Carmel (*off*) Hiya.

Doreen Hiya, love.

  Carmel comes in with a coat on and hood up. She's carrying bags of clothes, all marked separately.

Carmel Bloody teeming down.

Doreen Never seen rain like it.

She dumps the bags and takes her coat off, putting it on the back of a chair.

I've got you all set up.

Carmel Ta.

Carmel turns the iron on and goes into the kitchen.
    She comes back with a small plastic jug with water in and pours it into the iron.

Doreen Just made a fresh pot there.

Carmel goes back into the kitchen and makes herself a cup of tea.
    A ping from the kitchen from Carmel's phone.
    Doreen wraps the scarf carefully, checks the name and address and writes it on the package.
    A ping from Doreen's phone. She looks at it, smiles and texts a reply.
    Carmel comes back in with her cup of tea in one hand and phone in the other.
    She looks up above her to the room upstairs but doesn't say anything.
    She starts to work her way through bags of ironing, mainly shirts but dresses and blouses too – ironing each one carefully. She hangs each one up on a hanger in the door frame into the kitchen as she goes along. Gradually filling more of the door frame as the scene continues.
    Carmel looks at all Doreen's parcels.

Carmel You'll be a power seller soon.

Doreen I hope so. I do love it.

Pause.
    Doreen looks at all the bags of clothes to be ironed.

You've done well. So resourceful of you.

Carmel I had to do something didn't I. And this is just from the cards I put through doors this last week.

Doreen Did you just do the posh houses up the top?

Carmel Oh yeah. Who else has got the spare change round here for this?

Carmel and Doreen both work away in silence for a long time. Carmel ironing, Doreen wrapping.
Carmel's phone pings. She looks at it, replies and drinks some more of her tea.
They work some more.
Doreen's phone pings. She looks at it and replies.
She looks up above her.
A faint ping from upstairs.

Doreen Did you bring more clothes for her?

Carmel Yeah, in one of these bags here. Just a couple of things. (*Referring to the text.*) Was that her, Anne Frank? Can't she come down and speak to you?

Doreen She likes to text.

Doreen goes off to the kitchen.

Carmel What you doing?

Doreen (*poking her head back round the door frame*) She'd like a drink.

Carmel Has she got you waiting on her hand and foot?

Doreen makes Megyn an orange squash and heads upstairs with it.
Carmel listens to Doreen go upstairs and then walk across the landing above her.

Doreen (*off/faint*) Megyn? Love? (*She knocks on the door.*) I've got your orange squash you asked for. I'll leave it outside the door.

Carmel I don't fuckin' believe this.

Carmel takes her phone out and calls Megyn on her phone in the upstairs room.
She listens as it rings faintly upstairs.
Doreen comes back down the stairs.

(*Shouting above her.*) Answer your bloody phone!

Doreen comes back into the dining room.

She's not answering her phone.

Doreen Oh, she won't. Texting's best.

Carmel ends the call.
Doreen listens. They hear footsteps upstairs. Then the bedroom door open and close.

I think she's got it.

Doreen's phone pings. She reads the message.

Yeah, she's got it.

Doreen texts a reply.

Carmel This is cuckoo.

Doreen It's fine.

Carmel How much longer is she gonna be here? It's been three bloody weeks now.

Doreen Let's see what happens. Are you missing her?

Carmel I'm grateful for the peace.

They both get back to their jobs and continue as they talk.

Are you still sleeping on the sofa?

Doreen It's more comfortable than it looks.

Carmel It's not right she's taken over your room and bed.

Doreen I like having her here. It's nice.

Carmel You're as cracked as her.

47

Doreen It's so long since you two went and your dad . . . She's keeping me company.

Carmel From a closed room on another floor?

Doreen We've got our little routines. She'll text me if she's hungry or wants anything. Or I'll say, 'Fancy an orange squash?' And she'll send me a thumbs up.

Carmel (*sarcastic*) Aw.

Doreen I'm up to speed on most of what she'll eat. She is quite fussy though isn't she. I buy her what she likes now and I'm happy to cook something separate for her. She sends me interesting videos to watch and funny things. And vice versa.

Carmel You're both as bad as one another.

Doreen Some of it goes right over my head but she is a teenager. I am still a bit worried about her. I think she's still frightened . . .

Carmel Has she actually said that?

Doreen She doesn't need to, I can just tell.

Carmel And what the hell is she frightened of?

Doreen She doesn't say. Maybe it is this environment stuff. If she thinks we're all about to die . . .

Carmel I'll end her world.

Doreen Or maybe something *has* happened to her.

Carmel She's enjoying all the fuss she's making.

Doreen She is terrible with her phone. She's always either on it or me iPad or both at the same time. I thought you were bad with your phone but it's like it's her job. She's sat there poised for anything coming in, responding immediately. Who's she talking to?

Carmel Who knows? Paedophiles in America?

48

Doreen And now she doesn't even like me going in there. I have to leave stuff outside the door and then scarper.

Carmel It's like you're in a zoo and feeding some rare marsupial.

Doreen She's only been doing that the past couple of days. Before, I could go in.

Carmel Has she been out of that room since she went in there?

Doreen Only to use the bathroom.

Carmel She doesn't come down? This is madness.

Doreen If I haven't heard a peep out of her in a while, I just check to see if she's posted anything or if she's active online, then I know she's okay.

There's movement upstairs. They both look up.
Pause.

Carmel Oh yeah, she is still alive.

Doreen Stop that.

Carmel Have you seen the garbage she posts? What is it today? Let's have a look. (*She looks at her phone and reads.*) 'A mother's hug lasts long after she lets go.' She's taking the piss now. (*Half shouting above her.*) You're taking the piss now.

Doreen I thought that was nice, that one.

Carmel It'd be fine if she was actually talking to me. She posts all these pictures of me and her as a baby . . . Where is she getting these photos from?

Doreen They're mine. She found a load of old pictures in boxes upstairs.

Carmel She's putting all these photos of us together with dickhead quotes and she's getting all these stupid comments . . . (*She looks at her phone.*) 'I wish I had a relationship like that with my mum,' off that witch from Superdrug, and, 'Real

49

mother-daughter love,' from . . . (*She looks again.*) 'Sofia', some random girl in Germany. But she's practically moved out and isn't friggin' speaking to me. I feel like throwing this away sometimes. (*Holding up her phone.*) Everyone's so angry and political. It used to be nice. When it was just baby photos and pictures of your dinner. But now. You can't say anything to anyone. Everyone's screaming at each other. 'You're wrong, I'm right.' 'I'm offended.' 'You're a Fascist.' 'You're a Nazi.'

Doreen Have you seen Sarah's all over it now?

Carmel Since this new head at the school, she thinks everything's about the environment or politics. Even when someone posts a nice picture of their holidays, she goes off on one.

Doreen (*half whispered*) Has Megyn got many friends?

Carmel She's got two thousand online but in reality, none.

Doreen (*whispered*) Doesn't she see any of the girls from school?

Carmel She doesn't see anyone. (*Whispered.*) You don't need to whisper.

Doreen What about that Kimberley?

Carmel Naah. And it turns out she was a right cow.

Doreen Wasn't there a boy? That one that she liked.

Carmel Oh yeah, Brook or Bronk or something.

Doreen Weren't they going out with each other?

Carmel I think so. She really liked him. Was spending all her time with him, then nothing. Don't know what happened there.

Doreen Maybe he did something to her . . .

Carmel Maybe? Who knows? She's not telling me anything.

Doreen You know she sleeps with the phone in her hand?

Carmel These bloody things.

Her phone pings. She looks at it and texts a quick reply.

I do hate them but if I didn't have this as a constant distraction I might stop and realise how shite my life really is.

Doreen picks her iPad up off the table and searches for something.

Doreen Ee are, you should see what she's been looking at on me iPad.

Doreen shows Carmel.

Carmel She didn't clear her history? Amateur.

Carmel reads.

Doreen See?

She scrolls through.

What d'you make of that?

Carmel reads some more.

Carmel She's left that on there for you to see. She's no more trans than I am.

Doreen You sure? There's pages and pages and pages of it.

Carmel Naah.

Doreen She did get that short haircut a while ago. And I can't remember the last time I saw her in a nice skirt.

Carmel She wishes she was different or interesting but she's not. She doesn't know who she is. How to be.

Doreen And this . . . (*She searches.*) Now this . . . Where is it? This is . . .

She finds what she's looking for and passes the iPad to Carmel.

Look. I never knew there was all this stuff out there. Horrific.

Carmel reads.

Carmel She's such a cliché.

Doreen Self-harm. Aren't you worried?

Carmel She won't be doing any of that, she's too much of a wuss.

Doreen I could hardly sleep last night when I saw that.

Carmel She's got you right under her spell.

Doreen Don't be daft. She does look at some weird things. Serial killers. She loves them.

Carmel I do like a bit of true crime meself. We used to watch those together. We really bonded once over a ten-part series about the Moors Murders.

Doreen And the news. She loves the news. When I was seventeen, I wasn't keeping up to date on what was going on all over the world. And she's still unhappy about the broadband. Says it's not fast enough.

Carmel How fast does she want it? What the hell's she doing up there?

Doreen I think it's so she can stream films.

Carmel Or organise terrorist plots.

They both go back to their work.
Doreen's phone makes a 'ker-ching' cash register sound.
She picks up her phone and looks at it.

Doreen Another sale. That's my favourite sound in the world. Just sold one of me old dresses.

Carmel It is quiet at home.

Doreen See, you are missing her.

She finishes ironing a shirt and hangs it in the door frame.

Carmel The other night I did get a bit freaked out. I was lying in bed scrolling through the holiday photos of someone

I hardly know, when I just got . . . This shiver came over me . . . I put the covers over me like I was hiding from something . . .

Doreen That's not like you.

Carmel I was just lying there under the covers terrified all of a sudden . . .

Doreen Of what?

Carmel I don't know. Some sort of nameless dread. I was practically shaking. And I didn't know why. Then I got it in me head that there was something downstairs.

Doreen A burglar?

Carmel Not someone. Something.

Doreen Were you drunk?

Carmel After a bit I plucked up the courage and went downstairs with that bit of broken-off banister in me hand. And did lots of grunting and shuffling like there was a load of us upstairs, and we were all big burly men . . .

Doreen And?

Carmel Nothing. Nothing there.

Doreen D'you remember that time Pat Jones was burgled while she was in bed and they'd heated up big pans of water on her stove, in case she came down, to throw over her?

Carmel Then when I was downstairs, I thought there was something upstairs. Not a burglar but something . . . A thing. A shape.

Doreen You must have been drunk. Had you been drinking?

Carmel Not really, no. I don't know what was going on. But I was too scared to go back up. I ended up sleeping on the sofa. I took two antihistamines and put a chair against the door, just in case.

Doreen You should have called me.

Carmel You've got enough on your plate.

Doreen It's because you're missing her up there. It is.

Carmel's phone pings. She looks at it and responds. She scrolls through.
Doreen goes back to her packaging.
Carmel is lost in her phone for a few moments.

Carmel Look at this. Bloody picture of me holding her at her christening.

Doreen looks.

Doreen Ah. Look at your hair there.

Carmel 'The best mum in the world.'

Doreen I think it's her reaching out to you. She knows you're here.

Carmel Why doesn't she come down then?

Doreen Have you asked her to come home?

Carmel She knows where she lives. Tried calling and it just rings out. I'm not gonna beg.

Doreen Maybe if you posted a nice comment?

Carmel For everyone to see?

Doreen Why not?

Carmel I've got to play some public game and pretend we get on?

Doreen Give it a try. It makes it more real then, doesn't it.

Carmel It's only real if everyone knows about it?

Doreen I think she'd like it.

Carmel *(muttered under her breath)* It's all bloody stupid.

They go back to their respective jobs. Carmel ironing, Doreen packaging.
Sarah comes in through the back door.

Sarah (*off*) Hiya. Hello.

Doreen looks into the kitchen.

Doreen Leave your brolly in there.

She comes into the dining room. She has a mac on. She takes it off and puts it onto the back of a chair.

Sarah It's starting to stop. I've got half an hour of dinner before I go back in to the little cherubs.

Doreen There was some tea, but you'll probably want to make some fresh.

Sarah Oh okay.

Sarah looks up above her to where Megyn is.

(*To Doreen, quiet.*) How's . . .?

Doreen points at Carmel and shakes her head.

Doreen Shush.

Sarah (*to Carmel*) What's all this about?

Carmel Didn't me mum tell you? You know friendly Boots, who you can trust? Why go to a doctor when you can go to Boots? Who I've been working for, for twenty years.

Sarah Oh, did the new contracts go through?

Carmel takes a dress out of a bag and starts ironing it.

Carmel It wasn't enough halving my hours to part time. Oh no, my new 'flexible contract' has started. 'More flexibility for me and more flexibility for Boots.' Well, actually no flexibility for me, just Boots can do whatever they want. I'm on a friggin' zero-hours contract. 'There won't be much change to your hours, we just want to respond to the changing nature of retail.' As in, no one's coming into Town any more and especially not in the week.

Doreen Town's not the same since Marksies closed.

Sarah It's so sad.

Carmel Couple that with the automatic tills and there'll be no jobs left soon. And guess what, it's mainly us women who were doing these jobs. Male bosses still happy as Larry but all the female shop workers are buggered. So, no regular income. And only more reliant on this . . . (*She holds up her phone.*) As they're gonna text me of a morning if they want me to go in or not.

Sarah Can they just do that?

Carmel They can do whatever they want. So, bring on more of this, for lazy men . . .

She looks at the dress she's ironing.

. . . and women . . . who can't be arsed ironing their own clothes.

She hangs the dress up in the doorway.

All to keep a roof over her head, even though she's not living with me . . .

Sarah What does your union say?

Carmel No one's in a union. Of course, we're not.

Sarah goes over to the sideboard and looks at the packaged parcels.

Sarah Look at this . . .

Doreen Don't touch. It's all in order.

Sarah Where do you get all this from?

Doreen Some of it's mine, stuff from around the house, and some of it I've bought in second-hand shops or online and I sell it on.

Sarah Proper little capitalist.

Carmel You what?

Doreen It's just something to do. I love this bit. Parcelling them all up and sending them on their way.

She looks at the pile of items to be wrapped.

Sarah Is this all sold?

Doreen Yes, leave them alone.

Sarah Wasn't this Operation game mine? Have you sold it?

Doreen Probably. And yes. Do you still want it?

Sarah Ah I loved it. Does it still work?

Doreen I put new batteries in to check and it's fine.

Sarah Can't believe you've sold it.

Carmel Has it got deep sentimental value for you?

Sarah (*to Doreen*) What if I wanna keep it?

Doreen Make up your mind because I'm wrapping it next.

Sarah I suppose I can let it go.

Carmel Do you wanna say your final goodbyes?

Doreen You haven't touched it in thirty years.

Sarah It'll be nice to think of some kid playing with it somewhere.

She picks up a small screwdriver set.

Wasn't this screwdriver set me dad's?

Doreen Hmmm yeah.

Sarah And you're selling it? And this chess set was his.

Doreen Can you just leave it all alone?

Doreen finishes wrapping a parcel and writes the address on the front. She places it with the other packaged items.

Sarah But it was me dads'.

Carmel Well, he's not here to use it, is he.

Sarah I know but . . .

Doreen It's all just been sitting there gathering dust for years. I've told you many times to take anything you want.

Sarah It's fine.

Sarah heads into the kitchen to put the kettle on. We hear her filling the kettle up.
Doreen takes the Operation game and wraps it forcefully.
Carmel hangs up a shirt she's ironed in the door frame.

(*Shouting through.*) We all up for a fresh cup?

Doreen Ooh yeah.

Carmel Go on then.

Sarah leans in the door frame while she waits for the kettle to boil.

Sarah Me and Simon have just booked a holiday for the summer holidays. We're going to Cuba.

Carmel You're going away with him already?

Sarah Very spur of the moment. We were talking about places we wanted to go to, he's big into travel, next minute we're booking a trip to Havana. It's great to be so spontaneous. I've always wanted to go.

Doreen Have you?

Sarah Oh yeah. He's done lots of Latin America but not Cuba.

Doreen Pat McMahon went with their Maureen didn't she. Said the food was terrible. Nothing fresh. Couldn't find a tomato anywhere for love nor money.

Carmel Must cost a bit. Is he paying for it?

Sarah We're going halves. I wouldn't want him to pay for it. Even though he does earn a lot more than me. I'm gonna put it on a credit card. Why not? Life's short.

Carmel Isn't flying bad for the environment?

Sarah Only if you do it loads.

She sits down at the table, takes her phone out and scrolls through it.

I can't quite believe we've found each other. He was only meant to be up in Birkenhead temporarily, but he loves it so much he's really thinking of staying for good.

She drifts off slightly into her own world.

You know what, he's just thoughtful and kind . . .

The kettle boils in the kitchen. It has a whistle on it and starts whistling. Sarah doesn't move. She's looking at her phone. Doreen moves.

Doreen Kettle's boiling. Shall I go and . . .?

Sarah Oh, go on then.

Doreen goes through to the kitchen.
Sarah's phone pings.

This is him now. 'Just thinking about you.' Whenever I'm talking about him, he messages. How weird is that?

Carmel Well, if you're always talking about him and he's always texting you, then the chances are pretty high.

Carmel focuses on her ironing.
Sarah types a reply.

Sarah 'Was just telling family about holiday. They're really pleased.' He's been everywhere. He does a lot of work Down Under. He was telling me how amazing New Zealand is. He said we should go and live there the other night.

Carmel I've heard it's just like North Wales.

Doreen (*shouting through*) You'd move away from here?

Sarah I don't know. Just a crazy thought. There's not much keeping me here apart from youse lot.

Doreen appears at the door to the kitchen.

Doreen And your job. It's a long way to go. I'd want you to do anything that made you happy. That's the most important thing.

Doreen goes back into the kitchen.

Sarah I do love me job. Now that Felicity's here. I'm fired up every morning. There could be an amazing school in New Zealand. Let's see what happens.

Carmel How's your new bike?

Sarah I haven't sorted it yet.

Carmel I thought cars were banned?

Sarah Soon.

Doreen (*poking her head round the kitchen door*) She's been parking it in the back here and walking round. When she can get a spot. So they don't know she's driven.

Sarah Shush. I'll get a bike soon.

Doreen enters from the kitchen with a tray in her hands. On the tray there's a teapot, three cups, milk jug, sugar bowl and three Orange Club biscuits in their wrappers.

Doreen (*with a jolly sing-song delivery*) Tea's made. Found some Club biscuits too.

Carmel Oh Mum.

Doreen places the tray on the table. She gives the tea a good stir. Then pours three cups of tea and adds milk.

Doreen It'd be nice to meet this Simon with the lovely teeth.

Sarah You will. I was gonna bring him round today, but he's chocka at work.

Carmel Hmmm.

Sarah He'd love to meet you all. I've told him everything about you.

Doreen finishes pouring the tea.

Doreen There you go. This one's a bit weak.

Carmel I'll have it.

She passes Carmel a tea.

Ta, Mum.

Then another to Sarah.

Doreen You like a strong one.

Sarah Ta.

Carmel adds two spoonfuls of sugar to her tea. Doreen adds a half.
Carmel stops ironing. She sits at the table, drinks her tea and looks at her phone.
Doreen sits at the table, drinks her tea and looks at her phone.
Sarah looks at her phone.
Carmel and Doreen take a Club biscuit and eat it with their tea.
Pause. They all look at their phones.
Doreen's phone makes a new alert sound. She watches closely.

Doreen Ooh.

It makes the same sound.

Ooh yeah.

Carmel and Sarah look at each other.

Sarah You alright, Mother?

Her phone makes the sound again.

Doreen It's one of me auctions coming to an end. They wait until the last few moments and then all start frantically outbidding each other. I love it. (*She looks back to her phone.*) Ten seconds.

Her phone makes the sound twice in quick succession.

Come on.

Her phone makes the sound once more. Then a final different sound.

And we're done.

Sarah Bonkers.

Carmel Whatever floats your boat.

Her phone makes a cash register ker-ching sound.

Doreen Sold. So, I've made . . . (*Thinking to herself.*)
I bought it for . . . Take a couple of quid for postage . . .
I've made seventeen pounds. That's good that.

Sarah Can you be arsed doing all that for seventeen quid?

Doreen Of course I can be arsed. It's money I didn't have
before and it's better than nothing. And I enjoy it.

Sarah What time is it? (*She looks at the time on her phone.*)
I'd better get back soon. Oh, I had the most awful day
yesterday. Had another kid taken into care. I shouldn't really
tell you any of this . . .

Carmel gets up and goes back to her ironing.

We were doing baking. Some dead-easy fairy cakes with the
Year Threes, they're seven . . . And this gorgeous little girl,
I won't say her name . . . I pass her the wooden spoon and
tell her to mix all the ingredients together and she says,
'Mummy hits me with a wooden spoon.'

Doreen Oh, she didn't.

Sarah I just went, 'Okay, you come with me, lovely.' And
I took her out of class and to our head of safeguarding, who
is also the head, Felicity. And I just said, 'You tell Miss
Barker-White what you told me.' And she said the same thing
again. Felicity asked her to show her where and she pointed

to her backside. You've got to be so careful. You can't ask any leading questions. You're not even allowed to take off any of their clothes and look. Felicity was brilliant. Made it all low key and chatty, you don't want it to feel like a drama or scare the kid cos they'll just shut down. Then she called all the authorities, social services, the police blah blah blah. The worst bit is she then has to call the mum and say, 'Your daughter has made an allegation and you need to come into school.' And all hell breaks loose.

Doreen This is what you have to deal with?

Sarah Usually, it happens at the end of day on the last Friday before the summer holidays, when they don't want to go home for the long break. That's when they say something. They were all there until ten o' clock last night and she didn't go home with her mum. She's now in foster care. Apparently, she had bruises all . . .

She gestures towards her bottom.

Doreen Don't, Sarah.

Carmel But what happens if they're lying?

Doreen What child would lie about something like that?

Carmel Kids do lie, make things up.

Sarah Sometimes they do. They don't know what they're saying. They've seen or heard something but maybe it hasn't happened to them. But even then, they might be getting exposed to things they shouldn't at such a young age. And that's abuse. Or they say something for some attention and it all gets out of hand. We're trained to always think the worst, which sounds mad. But a child saying something in passing could lead you to discovering a whole raft of issues.

Carmel Sounds perfect for a drama queen like you.

Sarah I'm not a . . . I'm just listening and acting on what's been said. Just cos you don't like to deal with anything.

Doreen And on this occasion, you did the right thing and hopefully the little kiddie's in a better place.

Sarah There'd been a few red flags before and apparently social services already had files on the mother. They're so poor, this family . . .

Doreen That's no excuse.

Sarah I know, I . . .

Doreen Just because people are poor doesn't mean you go round battering your children.

Sarah I wasn't saying that. The worst case of abuse Felicity's seen was from this millionaire family at her previous school where they had this cage in the basement and . . .

Carmel I don't wanna hear any more.

Doreen And some of these people who say they're poor. They don't know they're born. Bet you they've still got mobile phones and . . .

Sarah Okay, Mum.

Doreen Well.

> *Doreen goes back to her packaging.*
> *Sarah heads into the kitchen.*

Sarah Got anything else to munch on?

Doreen There's some ham there. And bread. And while I remember. You know some of this environmental stuff, they don't know if it's for real or not.

> *They continue to talk, half shouting through from one room to the other.*

Sarah I think the plastic in the oceans and animals on the verge of extinction is not made up.

Doreen Climate change could be something which happens naturally though. Some people think it might not be our fault.

Sarah Where did you get this from?

Doreen I just heard it . . . read it somewhere.

Sarah I think it is.

Doreen That's not what I've heard. There's another side of the story that often doesn't get mentioned. You're not always right you know, Sarah.

Sarah Okay, okay.

Doreen Well . . .

> *Pause.*
> *Sarah comes in with a ham sandwich on a small plate and a bag of crisps. She puts them on the table and sits down.*

Where did you get those crisps from?

Sarah In the cupboard.

Doreen They're not for . . .

> *Doreen swiftly takes the bag away and into the kitchen.*

Carmel Here we go.

> *Doreen comes back in and chucks a bag of crisps Sarah's way. She heads back to her packing.*

Doreen Have the salt and vinegar ones.

> *Sarah looks to Carmel confused.*

Carmel It'll be because the others are for the lunatic in the attic. (*Pointing upstairs.*) She doesn't like salt and vinegar.

> *Sarah eats the sandwich, crisps and drinks her tea.*
> *Doreen phone pings. She looks at it, gets up immediately and heads into the kitchen.*

Carmel That her again?

Doreen (*off*) No. It was someone else. About a sale.

Carmel You're such a bad liar. (*To Doreen.*) Then what are you doing?

Doreen (*off*) Just thought she might like a yogurt.

Carmel I don't believe this. Are you seriously . . .?

Doreen is at the doorway with a yogurt in one hand – with the lid removed – and a teaspoon in the other.

Doreen It's only a friggin' rhubarb yogurt.

She heads upstairs.

Carmel I'm glad you took the lid off for her. She'd have been well flummoxed. Although she won't be happy about that plastic pot! (*To Sarah.*) She's got her run ragged.

Sarah I think she's much happier here.

Carmel And what's that supposed to mean?

Sarah (*throwaway*) You know . . .

Doreen knocks on the bedroom door upstairs.

Carmel Listen to this.

They both listen out.

Doreen (*off, upstairs*) Got the rhubarb yogurt you asked for. I'll just leave it here.

Carmel Me mum's not even allowed in her own bedroom now. But then she's just as warped. She says she's enjoying all this.

Sarah But don't you sometimes think it'd be nice to climb back into your old bed upstairs and have me mum looking after you?

Carmel Like you're off school sick.

Sarah And she'd bring you Lucozade and Heinz tomato soup.

Carmel Shall we all go and join her?

Sarah I said I'd see Megyn when I came round. She wants to speak to me.

Carmel What about?

Sarah I'm not sure but she's said she feels she can tell me things she can't tell you.

Carmel Oh right. She said that?

Sarah Hmm yeah. That's partly why I've come round.

Carmel She's summoned you, has she?

Sarah She's gonna explain what this is all about.

Carmel She won't even open the door for y'.

Sarah She will. D'you think me mum's okay?

Carmel Apart from all this shenanigans, she's fine.

Sarah She seems to be getting more . . . opinionated.

Carmel Good on her.

Doreen comes back down the stairs and into the dining room. She gets back to her work.
Her phone pings. It's Megyn. She replies immediately.

Sarah I'll go and have a word.

Carmel (*sarcastic*) Good luck with that.

Sarah heads upstairs.
Carmel and Doreen continue to work.
Sarah knocks on the door upstairs.
Carmel listens.

Sarah (*off*) Megyn, love. It's me, your Auntie Sarah . . . Are you there?

Carmel Oh, you know I hate asking . . . And I wouldn't ask but . . .

Doreen How much?

Carmel Just twenty quid until . . .

Doreen takes her purse, takes out two tenners and places them on the ironing board.

It's just until . . .

Doreen Shush.

Carmel Thanks, Mum.

Carmel puts the money in her pocket. Doreen has her back to the patio doors.
A man appears at the patio doors behind them.
Carmel sees him and screams.

What the friggin' frig? There's a man . . .

Doreen sees the man.

Doreen What the hell are you . . . ?

He disappears out of view.
Doreen rushes off to the kitchen to go and speak to him.
Carmel gets her breath back.

Carmel Bloody hell. I'm a nervous wreck. Who is it? What does he want?

Doreen (*off*) It's fine.

Carmel Scared the living daylights out of me.

Carmel moves towards the kitchen doorway to go and look. She gets caught up in the clothing hanging in the door and knocks some of them off.

Fuck, fuck. Who is it?

Doreen comes out of the kitchen.

Doreen It's fine, he's gone.

Carmel Who was he?

Doreen Wrong address.

Doreen goes back to her packaging.
Carmel picks up the ironing she's knocked off.

Carmel I'll have to do some of these again. What did he say?

Doreen Something about looking for . . . I don't know . . .
I sent him on his way.

Carmel I thought you knew him.

Doreen No.

Carmel goes back to the window and looks out.

Carmel He's gone now.

Doreen I know. I told you that.

Carmel You don't think it was a burglar casing the joint,
seeing if anyone was in?

Doreen Course not. What's there to steal? I think he meant
to go to the Avenue, we're always getting people mixing up
the Close and the Avenue.

Carmel Who did he ask for?

Doreen (*getting more irritated*) Oh I don't know. But he's
gone now so . . .

Carmel Just odd, don't you think?

Doreen Are you a bit on edge?

Carmel No. No.

*She has one more look out of the patio doors and goes
back to her ironing.*
*Doreen sends a text on her phone. She gets an almost
instant ping reply. She sharply texts again. Ping another
reply. She texts back with a huff and then puts her phone
to one side. She goes back to her wrapping.*

Doreen It's stopped raining.

Carmel So it has.

Doreen Looks like the sun's coming out.

Carmel Hmmm.

They continue with their chores. There's an intensity to their work.
Sarah comes back down the stairs and into the dining room.

Sarah She wouldn't open the bloody door.

Carmel laughs.
Sarah drinks the rest of her tea.

Doreen You've got to text her.

Sarah I did.

Carmel From the other side of the door? She's got us all behaving like lunatics.

Sarah She said now wasn't the right time to talk . . . It's fine. I understand. I really do think maybe something awful's happened to her.

Doreen Don't say that.

Sarah I just feel . . . The way she keeps on reaching out to me.

Carmel By not opening the door to you?

Sarah She sends me loads of messages saying she misses me. That she's sorry she hasn't taken me up on my offer at the school. I told her the offer's still open. Whenever she's ready. I remembered she did say a funny thing that first night she went in there. Well, not funny, just . . .

Carmel (*impatient*) What did she say?

Sarah That she misses Grandad. Me dad. I suppose it's not that odd.

Carmel It is a bit. He died, what, four years ago now. She's never really mentioned him since he . . .

Sarah Maybe that's what this is all about.

Carmel I doubt it.

Sarah And she said, what was it? 'Changing. Changing . . .'

Carmel Changing? What's changing?

Sarah Dunno. Maybe climate change.

Doreen Or she's changing?

Carmel Into what? She's really milking her part now.

Sarah I just hope she's not gonna do anything stupid.

Doreen Well . . .

Carmel This is all stupid.

Sarah (*to Doreen*) What does that mean?

Doreen She googled 'self-harm' . . .

Sarah She didn't?

Carmel She also googled Fred West but I don't think that makes her a serial killer.

Sarah This is different.

Carmel She did it on me mum's iPad, she wanted her to see. If she was serious, she'd have done it on her own phone. Which I pay for by the way.

Doreen She's fine. I'm looking after her. You don't need to worry.

Sarah Apparently, lots of young people are doing it. You know we'd all be trying cigarettes when we were kids? This is the new smoking.

Doreen Oh, that's awful.

Sarah I was telling Simon about all this and he was horrified. Couldn't believe we hadn't got the doctor out to see her.

Doreen D'you think we should?

Sarah Yes.

Carmel There's people with cancer who can't get treatment. They'll have no time for a teenager who's in a bit of a mood.

Sarah I was thinking . . . D'you think she might be on the spectrum? You know, autistic, neurodivergent . . .

Doreen You what?

Sarah Just the way she is sometimes. Being so quiet, almost non-verbal . . .

Carmel She's a teenager.

Sarah And other things. Not having many friends, becoming obsessive about stuff . . . And the way she is with food . . .

Carmel She's a fussy teenager.

Sarah I think you need to take this more seriously.

Carmel I wish you'd stop getting all worked up by her. This is exactly what she wants.

The sound of Megyn moving about upstairs.
They all stop what they're doing and look up.
They all listen.
The movement continues.

Sarah What's she doing?

Doreen Shush.

More movement.

Carmel Probably just getting the chair ready under the noose.

Doreen You've gone too far now.

Sarah Imagine how you'll feel if something awful happens.

They all stand stock-still and listen some more.
More movement above, then silence.
Pause.
Carmel's phone pings. She looks at it. Smiles and replies.
Sarah's phone pings.

Ah that's Simon. Asking if we should go out for tea.

She replies.
    Doreen goes back to her packaging.
    Carmel continues with her ironing.
    The moment has passed.

Shit, I'd better go back to school.

She puts her coat on, picks up her Club biscuit.

You can't beat a Club biscuit.

She rushes out through the kitchen.

See you later. T'ra.

Doreen T'ra, love.

Carmel starts ironing a new shirt. Doreen wraps another item to sell. They both work away in silence for a long time.
    Long pause.
    Doreen's phone pings. She looks at it.

She's fine.

Carmel doesn't say anything but rolls her eyes.
    Doreen goes out to the kitchen.
    We hear Doreen moving about in the kitchen. Then going upstairs.
    Carmel continues to iron.
    We hear a knock on the bedroom door.

(*Off.*) Megyn, love. I'll leave it outside for you.

Carmel continues to iron.
    Lights fade.
    End of Act Two.
    Possible interval.

Act Three

Dining room as before.
  Two weeks later.
  Daytime.
  It's a very sunny and hot spring day.
  The patio doors are open. The sun shines through.
  Doreen is out in the garden watering her potted plants on the patio.
  Her phone sits on the table and is playing 'Private Dancer' by Tina Turner. Doreen is singing along to the first verse of the song, outside. She knows all the words. We can't see her at first.
  There's a new lightness to Doreen.
  Doreen passes by the window. She's in her dressing gown and slippers with curlers in her hair. She goes back and forth as she waters the plants, singing the second verse.
  Doreen comes in through the patio doors with the watering can, and now sings along to the chorus. She waters the plants in the dining room.
  After that, she takes the watering can into the kitchen, now singing the two lines about a million dollars and the sea.
  She then comes back in with a face mirror on a stand.
  She hums along to the verse about a husband and some children as Tina Turner keeps singing.
  Doreen sits at the table where the light streaming in through the patio doors is particularly good.
  She turns the mirror over so it's on the side with the extreme magnification.
  She takes a pair of tweezers out of her dressing gown pocket and starts plucking small hairs out of her chin in the mirror.
  Her phone pings.

She stops humming. The song continues to play underneath.
She reads the text.
She looks up above her. It's from Megyn.
She goes to reply but pauses. She thinks for a second, then puts the phone down and carries on with her tweezering.
Doreen sings along again to the verse about Deutschmarks or dollars. She really likes this bit and really gets into it.
Doreen's phone rings. 'Single Ladies' by Beyoncé. 'Private Dancer' stops playing.
Doreen picks up her phone to see who's calling. She smiles and answers quickly.

Doreen (*into phone*) Hello you . . . (*She giggles.*) Of course I am. I'm just getting ready . . .

She looks up above her to where Megyn is.

What do you think? . . . I know, you're right . . . I've had enough now . . . No, no, you are right . . . I just need to get out . . . I'm looking forward to seeing you too . . . (*She giggles again.*) Okay, Poodle . . . See you in a bit . . . T'ra . . .

She puts the phone down and gets back to the mirror.
Carmel appears in the back garden in amongst the pots.
She storms into the dining room through the open patio doors. She's in her Boots uniform.

Carmel Is she in? Of course she's in. Where else is she gonna be?

She goes through to the kitchen.
Doreen doesn't get up. She continues plucking hairs out.

(*Shouting upstairs, off.*) Get down here now.

She comes back into the dining room.

I'm fuming.

Doreen I can see that.

Carmel Do you have to do that here?

Doreen The light's best here. And this is my house.

Carmel I'm furious.

Doreen (*busy tweezering*) I'd be very surprised if she comes down.

Carmel Have you seen what she's been putting? She's really lost it now. (*Shouting up, she doesn't move into the kitchen.*) If you don't come down, then I'm coming up.

Movement from the bedroom upstairs.

Oh, ee are. Listen.

They listen.
We hear a heavy piece of furniture being moved upstairs.

What's she doing? Moving the bed? (*Shouting up.*) What are you doing up there?

Doreen God only knows.

Carmel Right.

Carmel heads into the kitchen and upstairs.
We hear her footsteps as she goes upstairs.
Doreen goes back to calmly plucking.
She hums 'Private Dancer' to herself.
We hear hammering at the door upstairs.

(*Off.*) Have you locked this? Open this door now.

Carmel bangs on the door.

(*Off.*) I'll bash it down. You know I will. Open it now.

Carmel heads back down the stairs.
She comes back into the dining room.

It's locked. How's it locked? I didn't know there was a lock on your bedroom door.

Doreen There isn't.

Doreen has finished plucking and goes into the kitchen.

Carmel I think she's put a chair or chest of drawers behind the door. Like she's in a friggin' Tom and Jerry cartoon. (*Shouting up.*) I'll smash the door down. I will.

Doreen comes back in with a very old make-up bag. She's had it for years.
She turns the mirror over to the normal side and starts applying make-up – foundation, powder, blusher, mascara, eye shadow, lipstick. In the same way she always has since she was young.
Carmel is almost oblivious.

Have you seen what she's been posting?

Carmel takes her phone out and scrolls through.

This. This morning. (*Reading.*) 'A daddy will always be his daughter's first love.' Pass the sick bucket. With some awful photo of a girl and her father walking along a beach holding hands. Or this. (*Reading.*) 'The reason why daughters love their dads the most is because there's at least one man in the world who will not hurt her.' Oh yeah, the man who disappeared in the middle of the night over two years ago and hasn't paid a penny towards her upkeep since.

Doreen At least she's stopped writing crap about you.

Carmel scrolls through more.

Carmel Have you seen this one?

Doreen To be honest, I put her on mute on there the other day.

Carmel Maybe that's what I should do.

Doreen And I haven't actually seen her for a fortnight. She still won't open the door to me.

Carmel She penned this long monologue last night . . . (*Reading.*) 'Where are you, Dad? I hope you see this. If anyone knows him or sees him, can you get in touch?'

Doreen It's like she's looking for a missing cat.

Carmel It gets worse. (*Reading.*) 'The only person who understands me is my dad. Maybe if he was still around, I wouldn't be so screwed up.' Maybe I should tell her that one of the reasons he used to say he'd leave, was because of her. He couldn't stand the sight of her. Said she was a mistake that had trapped him with me . . . And then to make it all worse you've got messages from losers that she hardly knows. Oh, ee are, that horrible witch from Superdrug again, 'I'm sure he's looking for you, hun.' Is he buggery. 'He was a diamond your dad.' Oh, ee are, a new one she's written (*Reading.*) 'I'll always be my daddy's little girl and he will always be my hero.'

Doreen Maybe she's just trying to get a reaction.

Carmel Well she's got one hasn't she.

Doreen Just so you know. I'm going out soon.

Carmel Oh. Where?

Doreen Over to Liverpool.

Carmel All dickie dolled up like that?

Doreen Meeting Pat Smith. I just felt like making an effort.

Carmel scrolls through her phone.
Doreen's phone pings. She reads the message.

That's her now. 'Can I have some toast and butter please Nan?' At least she's rediscovered the word 'please'.

Carmel Don't you . . .

Doreen Don't worry. Enough. (*She texts and reads.*) 'You know where the kitchen is.'

Carmel Get you.

Doreen That might smoke her out.

She focuses on her make-up.
Carmel's phone pings. She looks at it quickly and reads.

78

Carmel Bloody Boots telling me to go in for one hour tomorrow. I'm putting it on silent.

Carmel flicks a switch to put her phone on silent. She goes into the kitchen. She shouts up.

I'm not leaving this house until you come down.

Sarah appears at the open patio doors.
She steps inside and stands in the doorway.
Her face is red and her eyes are watery.
Doreen looks up to see her.
Sarah tries to force out a smile.

Doreen Sarah?

She bursts out crying.

Sarah Oh Mum.

Doreen What's happened?

Doreen gets up and gives her a hug. Sarah cries into her.
Carmel comes back into the dining room. She sees Sarah.

Carmel This is all we need.

Carmel goes back into the kitchen and stomps up the stairs.

Doreen What is it?

Sarah cries some more.

Sarah He's gone.

Doreen Who?

She breaks apart from Doreen.

Sarah Simon! Who else?

She cries again.

Doreen Oh yeah, of course. Sorry.

Doreen passes Sarah the tissue box from the sideboard.
Carmel bashes on the bedroom door upstairs.

Carmel (*off*) You've got to come out sometime.

Doreen Where's he gone?

Sarah I don't know. He's just disappeared.

Sarah sits down at the table. She wipes her eyes and blows her nose.

Carmel (*off*) You can't stay in there forever.

Doreen (*half to herself*) Oh yes, she can. Let me get you a drink.

Sarah Got any orange?

Doreen I've got squash in for . . .

She points upstairs.

Sarah And anything chocolatey?

Doreen goes off to the kitchen.
Sarah stares ahead blankly.
She takes her phone out and looks at it. She's waiting for a message. Nothing.
She chucks it onto the table and puts her head in her hands.

I just don't know what's happened.

She talks louder so Doreen can hear in the kitchen.

We had a lovely night the other night. I cooked dinner, had a few drinks blah blah blah . . . He stayed over at mine. I went off to work and he said he had some things to do. I texted him later and there was no reply. I've texted him, called him, but it just says this number is unavailable.

Doreen pokes her head round the door.

Doreen You don't think something awful's happened, do you?

Sarah I hope not. That's what I keep thinking. It's so scary. Thinking of all the horrible things that could have happened to him. That he was run over or mugged or stabbed . . . or he's fallen down a ditch . . . I've called round all the hospitals, and the police, but there's no sign of him.

Doreen comes back in with an orange squash and a Penguin biscuit in a wrapper.

Doreen Found some Penguins.

She hands them to Sarah.

Sarah You're a star.

She drinks the squash and eats the Penguin.
Doreen sits down in front of the mirror and continues to do her make-up.

Doreen Have you been to his place?

Sarah Well, no . . . We never went to his house . . . He's got the builders in and said it was all just rubble and taking much longer than expected blah blah blah . . . You know what builders are like.

Doreen Not really, no. Where does he live?

Sarah I think it was Claughton Village.

Doreen You think? And you were talking of running off to New Zealand with him?

Sarah And Cuba. I'd paid the deposit. Does any of that matter now?

Her phone pings. She picks it up, full of hope.

Oh God . . . (*She looks at the message.*) Fuckin' Felicity, go away. Did I tell you she's leaving? Going off to run some posh private boarding school in York. I couldn't believe it. After everything she said about state schools and how they were what this country was built on. And after turning the school upside down on some stupid bloody green mission.

Doreen Have you tried his work?

Sarah looks at her mum. She pauses.

You don't know where he worked?

Sarah shakes her head.

Sarah He was a like a locum or something, so he wasn't based at one place. He was helping out at various . . .

She chucks her phone back on the table.

Was that all a load of . . . Was any of it real? He told me he loved me. We talked about marriage. Was he even a dentist?

Doreen With his lovely teeth? I'm sure he was.

Sarah We were having such a great time. Did I do something wrong? I thought everything was going really well. D'you think he just had enough of me and that's it? I really thought we'd spend the rest of our lives together . . . Oh Mum . . .

She starts to cry again.
  Doreen puts down her make-up and gets up to comfort her.

Doreen Oh love . . . He might have just . . . lost his phone . . .

Sarah (*hopeful*) D'you think?

Doreen Maybe yeah. And once he gets a new one, he'll be straight back onto you. Or it's ran out of power and he can't find a charger.

She thinks about it for a second and starts crying again.

Sarah Who am I kidding? We did have our first row . . . It wasn't really a row. He was saying how weird he found it . . . the whole thing with Megyn . . . That he couldn't believe we – I hadn't done more for her . . .

Doreen It's not really any of his business, is it.

Sarah Well, no, but it is weird, a teenager locking herself in her grandmother's bedroom . . . and I think he was just concerned. I got all defensive and it all got . . . But we made up in the end. I thought we had. Do you think he's dumped me because of that?

Doreen If he has, then good riddance.

Sarah Don't be like that, Mum.

Sarah looks up above her.

Is she still . . .?

Doreen (*snappy*) Yeah.

Carmel comes back in.

Carmel Let me guess. Has What's-his-face dumped you?

Doreen Carmel.

Doreen goes back to her make-up.

Carmel He'll be married, to at least two different women for sure. When are you gonna get the memo that no man is gonna save you?

Sarah Don't start.

Carmel You think you're some big political feminist but you want Prince Charming to come and whisk you away on a white horse.

Sarah I'm just optimistic. Well, I was . . .

Carmel Deluded.

Sarah I've got to be hopeful, otherwise . . .

Carmel You realise everything is shit.

Sarah Where are the good men? Men like me dad, eh?

Doreen Well . . .

Carmel All dead.

Sarah Why have I always had such bad luck with men?

Carmel Oh God.

Sarah At least I've got my family. We get on. Most of the time. Some people want nothing to do with their family. Can't be around them. (*She scrolls through her phone.*) I almost wish it was a scam. That he wanted a load of money off me. Rather than he just doesn't want to see me again.

Doreen You are talking rubbish now.

Carmel paces up and down.

Carmel (*to Doreen*) You still got that ladder in the garage? I could climb up and . . .

Sarah (*almost snapping out of it*) Right, we need to sort this out. Shall I go and speak to her?

Carmel *and* **Doreen** No.

Sarah It's gone too far now. I can't believe you're not doing more.

Doreen I called the doctor's.

Carmel You didn't. What did you do that for?

Sarah What did they say?

Doreen They don't really do house visits unless someone is close to death. They said bring her down to the clinic. We could have an appointment in a couple of weeks.

Carmel There you go.

Doreen I asked her if she'd come but she said she wanted to think about it. I actually think she's fine. She'll get bored and come out soon.

Carmel If I don't get her out of there first.

Sarah Maybe what's she doing is a perfectly rational response to what's going on in the world. I mean, look at this weather. It is lovely but it shouldn't be this hot in April.

Doreen continues to apply her make-up.
Carmel sees Sarah busy on her phone.

Carmel Are you just gonna sit and look at your phone?

Sarah Yeah. Maybe he'll . . .

Carmel (*she has an idea*) I know.

Carmel dashes off through the kitchen and into the hall.
Doreen continues with her make-up.
Pause.
Sarah looks up above her.

Sarah What if she is just having us all on?

Sarah finally clocks the make-up Doreen is putting on.

You going somewhere special?

Doreen Over to Liverpool.

Sarah Like this?

Doreen Can't I make an effort once in a while?

Sarah You got a fancy man over there?

Doreen (*a touch sharp*) Don't be ridiculous.

Sarah Okay.

Doreen I'm meeting Pat Smith.

Sarah I've just seen Pat Smith down at the bottom shops. She didn't say she was seeing you. She said she was babysitting little Lewis for the day.

Doreen I meant Pat Jones.

Sarah You're going out with Pat Jones?

Doreen Yeah, yeah.

Sarah scrolls through her phone. She finds something on it.

Sarah She's just posted a picture of her in Llandudno with her knitting group.

Doreen Did she?

Sarah She'd better get her skates on if she's gonna meet you in Liverpool this afternoon. Maybe you meant Pat McMahon?

Doreen I meant Pat McMahon. That's who I meant.

Carmel comes back in.

Carmel Turned off the wifi. She'll be lost.

Sarah (*to Doreen*) What's this all about?

Doreen You've got all me confused. With this whole interrogation.

Sarah I was only asking why you were getting all dolled up. One minute it's Pat Jones, then it's Pat Smith, then it's Pat McMahon.

Doreen It's not my fault I've got three friends called Pat. It was a very popular name when I was growing up.

Carmel Will you leave me mum alone?

Sarah Me? I was only asking . . . But it's like she's losing the plot.

Doreen Well, she's not losing the plot. I'm not meeting Pat Smith or Pat Jones or Pat McMahon.

Sarah (*half under her breath*) I think we know that.

Doreen It's a man. I'm going to meet a man. Barry's his name. Barry. That's who I'm going to meet. Okay?

Sarah and Carmel are silenced by the strength of her answer. Doreen has finished her make-up. Through the next section, she calmly takes her rollers out, one by one, and puts them in a small bag.

Carmel Right, okay.

Sarah Why didn't you just say that?

Doreen I don't know. I thought you wouldn't approve.

Carmel Of course not. You can do whatever you want.

Doreen I'm just being silly.

Carmel Er, yeah.

Sarah Who is he? This Barry.

Doreen He's just a man. He lives in Port Sunlight.

Sarah And what does he want?

Doreen What d'you mean?

Sarah Why are you seeing him?

Doreen We're meeting for coffee. Then we might go and see a film. And then for something to eat. Or the other way round.

Sarah But why? I don't understand.

Carmel Is it like . . . a date?

Doreen Yeah. We're going on a date.

Sarah You what?

Doreen I suppose you'd call it a date.

Carmel (*with a half-laugh*) Okay.

Sarah Why would you . . . Where did you meet him? This Barry.

Doreen On me iPad. He sent me a Direct Message and we just got chatting. He's lovely.

Sarah And what do you know about him?

Doreen I've had the police do a background check on him.

Sarah (*uncertain*) Have you?

Doreen Don't be so stupid. I'm old enough not to be scared of strangers.

Sarah You can't go on a date.

Doreen You see, I knew this is what I'd get. You can go on dates but I can't?

Sarah It's different for me.

Doreen Is this because yours didn't work out? If you can't have a boyfriend then neither can I?

Carmel Hang on you two.

Doreen I'm still alive you know, and I've never felt better.

Sarah What about me dad?

Doreen He's dead, Sarah. He's been dead for four years.

Sarah There'll never be anyone like me dad. He'll never take the place of him.

Carmel Bloody hell, she's only going on a date.

Doreen I do love Barry. And Barry loves me.

Carmel Oh.

Sarah You hardly know him.

Doreen I've known him a couple of months.

Sarah Exactly.

Carmel Says the woman who was thinking of flitting off to the other side of the world with some bloke she just met.

Doreen I feel I know him more than I knew your dad.

Sarah You can't say that, you were married to me dad for forty-five years.

Doreen He says things to me your father never said. What he's thinking, how he feels. We're in touch all day long.

Sarah You don't know what you're saying.

Doreen I know what I'm doing.

Sarah I don't think you do.

Doreen loses it.

Doreen Don't you dare tell me I don't know what I'm doing. Don't you dare.

Sarah Mother, okay.

Doreen I've spent my whole life being told 'you don't know what you're talking about'. 'You don't understand.' Well, I can say or do what I bloody well like. Don't you dare tell me what I can and can't say.

Carmel Mum . . .

Doreen I'm not gonna put up with it any longer.

Sarah I'm just concerned, that's all.

Doreen Well, you've got no need to be. Barry's gonna look after me now. Barry lets me be me. Encourages me, supports me, loves me for who I am.

Sarah Just like me dad did.

Doreen's phone pings. She looks at it.

Doreen This is him now. I'll reply to him in a mo. Well, no he didn't actually. Everything was your dad's way or the highway.

Sarah (*almost with a laugh*) What?

Doreen Why do you think I never worked while your father was alive? Because he wouldn't let me. I had to look after the house, be a housewife, married to the house. I wasn't allowed to have me own money, only the housekeeping your father gave me every week.

Sarah Where's all this coming from?

Carmel It was different then, wasn't it.

Doreen It's about time I said what really went on.

Sarah You were both really happy.

Doreen I thought I was. What about all his strange rules and regulations? No fish and chips. No radios or music. No coleslaw in the house. No plants. This soap, that washing powder . . .

Carmel That was just him being fussy wasn't it?

Doreen And controlling me.

Sarah I don't know why you're saying this.

Doreen It's the truth.

Doreen finishes taking all her rollers out and brushes her hair.

Sarah How did we not know?

Carmel If it was so bad, why didn't you leave?

Doreen Because I loved him and I didn't know it was wrong. I was used to it. And women didn't leave. How could you leave when you had no way of supporting yourself?

Sarah Why have you never said . . .

Doreen And I wouldn't want to get on the wrong side of your father.

Sarah You were scared of him?

Doreen I just knew to do as he said.

Sarah You've gone too far now.

Carmel He was strict.

Sarah Yeah, but we weren't scared of him, were we?

Doreen's phone makes a cash register ker-ching sound.

Doreen There you go. Another sale. Why do you think I love me buying and selling so much? I've got me own money at last to do what I want with.

Sarah and Carmel are speechless.
A noise from upstairs.

Carmel Shush.

Carmel listens. A heavy chest of drawers is being moved in the upstairs bedroom.

It's alive.

Doreen Barry loves money and so do I now. Barry lets me have my own opinion about things. And he understands me.

Sarah Mother . . .

The creak of the bedroom door opening upstairs.

Carmel Is she coming out of her nest?

Doreen He encourages me to speak my mind. Tells me off if I say, 'I'm not sure.' He tells me to say what I want and speak up.

More movement upstairs.

Sarah Is this where you're getting all these funny opinions from?

Doreen Funny?

Sarah Climate change is a real thing you know.

Doreen Just because I don't agree with you doesn't mean it's wrong. Barry says there's always another side to every story. He likes to look for the opposite opinion. Even if he doesn't agree with it himself. He'll pick a topic and we'll each take a side and have a debate. It's so much fun.

Carmel Shush.

Footsteps can be heard coming down the stairs.
They all listen.

She's coming down. What do we do?

Doreen It's only your bloody daughter. And sometimes we do really disagree and that's fine, he lets me have my opinion and doesn't fall out with me.

Sarah How very evolved of you.

The footsteps reach the bottom of the stairs.

Carmel (*imitating Megyn*) 'Can you turn the wifi back on?!' That'll be what she wants.

> *Carmel looks towards the kitchen door.*
> *A strange-looking Megyn slowly appears.*
> *She's wearing one of Doreen's old summer dresses –*
> *which is far too big – and her feet are bare. She's stooped*
> *and her hair is a mess, partly over her face. She looks very*
> *odd.*
> *She stands in the doorway.*
> *Sarah lets out a gasp.*

Sarah Oh!

Carmel What the fuck?

Doreen Oh my.

Sarah Come here, sit down.

> *Sarah helps her into a chair.*

Carmel Mother!

Doreen What have I done now?

Carmel You were meant to be looking after her. She looks like a crazy person.

Doreen Don't blame me. She's your daughter.

Carmel (*to Megyn*) What's this you're wearing?

Doreen One of my old dresses.

Carmel Why? (*To Megyn.*) Why are you wearing your nan's dress?

> *Megyn doesn't answer. She looks at the floor.*

Doreen Can you believe I used to wear this? (*To Carmel.*) I wore it to your wedding.

Carmel Thanks for the reminder.

Doreen I was going to sell it soon. I think someone might buy it.

They talk about Megyn almost like she's not there.

Sarah She looks so pale.

Carmel She looks ill.

Doreen She hasn't been outside for over a month. Once she gets some sunlight on her skin . . .

Sarah (*to Doreen*) Has she eaten much lately? When did she last eat?

Doreen This morning, I took her up her cereal.

Sarah (*to Megyn*) Did you eat it?

Megyn looks at her blankly.

(*To Doreen.*) What's been going on here?

Carmel God only knows.

Doreen Don't all look at me.

Carmel She asked you for some toast earlier and you just ignored her.

Doreen I told her to come down. I've been making sure she eats. I've been bloody well feeding her all day and night.

Carmel It doesn't look like she's been eating it though does it.

Doreen She leaves the empty bowls and plates outside the door.

Carmel (*to Megyn*) Have you not been eating?

Megyn just looks at her.

Megyn? (*Getting wound up.*) Eh?

Sarah Don't shout at her.

Carmel She could have been throwing it down the toilet for all you know.

Doreen Why would she do that?

Sarah (*to Doreen*) What the hell has been going on here?

Doreen This is all my fault is it? What can I do if she doesn't want to see me? We message each other all day long. She hasn't said anything was wrong. I ask her if she's okay and she sends me a thumbs up or love hearts and kisses.

Sarah You could have done more.

Doreen She's sleeping in my bloody bed. I've been on the couch since she cuckooed her way into my room. If I want anything out of me room, I have to text her and she'll leave it outside the door for me. Me knickers and bras.

Carmel Whole thing is crazy.

Doreen goes over to Megyn.

Doreen Her hair's just in her face . . .

She pushes Megyn's hair off her face.

Let's get your hair out of your . . . See, that's better already. She could probably do with a bath. She's fine. You're fine, aren't you?

Megyn doesn't answer.

I've been looking after you, haven't I?

Sarah's phone pings.
Megyn reacts, almost micro-flinching at the noise.

Sarah Let me just see if that's . . . (*She checks her phone.*) No.

Doreen I'll do her something to eat. I've got some cheddar cheese. She eats cheddar cheese. A cheese butty.

Doreen goes off into the kitchen.
Sarah's phone pings again.
Megyn reacts again.

Carmel Can't you put your bloody phone away? It's making her jump.

Sarah It could be Simon.

Carmel I don't care who it is.

Sarah looks at her phone.

Sarah It's not . . . Oh God. A hundred and twenty people dead in a train crash in Brazil.

Carmel For fuck's sake.

Sarah puts her phone in her pocket.
Megyn realises she hasn't got her phone.

Megyn Phone? Where's me phone?

Carmel It must be upstairs.

Megyn I need it.

She moves to go upstairs to get it.

Carmel No, you don't.

Megyn I do. If I don't . . .

She starts breathing heavily.

Sarah I'll get it.

Sarah goes out and upstairs to get Megyn's phone.

Carmel Just sit down.

She sits her back down.

It's okay. Auntie Sarah's getting your phone. Relax now.

Carmel looks at her.

What the hell . . . ?

Megyn's breathing calms.

That's better.

Doreen comes in with a sandwich on a small plate and a glass of orange squash.

She places it on the table in front of Megyn.
Megyn just stares at the food.

Doreen There's some orange squash too. She likes this.
I bought it special for her.

Carmel You eat the butty and drink the squash.

Doreen (*gentler*) Go on, it'll do you good.

She just looks at the food.

Carmel Do you think you can eat something for me?

No response. Pause.

Doreen Crisps. She likes crisps. I'll put them in a bowl.
Crisps always taste nicer in a bowl.

Doreen dashes off to the kitchen.
Sarah comes back in with the phone.

Sarah I couldn't find it at first. You should see it in there. It's
a right state.

Sarah passes Megyn the phone.
*She grabs it quickly and looks at it. She replies to a text
message swiftly, almost as if they aren't there.*

Carmel You don't need to look at your phone now. Have
some food first.

*Doreen comes back in with crisps in a cereal bowl. She
places it in front of Megyn.*
They all watch her.

Doreen Walkers Roast Chicken. Your favourite.

Megyn's phone pings. She texts a message back quickly.
*She looks at her phone like she's waiting for another
message to come through.*

Sarah Leave your phone. See if you can eat some food for
Auntie Sarah. Go on. It'll make you feel better.

Megyn holds her phone close to her and cautiously eats a crisp with very tiny bites.

Well done. Go on, have another.

Megyn takes another crisp.

See, I'm good with her.

Carmel Don't start with all that crap.

Sarah How about a sandwich? Little bite.

Doreen (*to Sarah*) It's mild cheddar cheese.

Sarah (*to Megyn*) It's mild cheddar cheese.

Megyn picks up the sandwich – which has been sliced into four small sandwiches – and cautiously takes a bite.

That's good, lovely.

Carmel And have some juice.

She sips some orange squash.

Doreen Well done.

They all watch in silence as she takes another bite and drinks some more.
  They watch her eat and drink.
  For a long time.
  Long pause.

I think she's gonna be okay.

Carmel Oh, do you now?

Doreen She'll feel better after she's eaten that. I need to get changed.

Doreen picks up her make-up and roller bag, and goes out into the kitchen. We hear her going off upstairs.

Sarah Is she still going out after all this?

Carmel is watching Megyn.

Carmel (*whispered to Sarah*) What do I do?

Sarah Maybe we really should get the doctor?

Carmel And say what?

Sarah She's not right.

Carmel (*to Megyn*) You feeling better for some food?

> *She doesn't respond.*
> *Carmel starts to get upset.*

What the hell . . .

Sarah Don't be getting all . . .

Carmel Look at her.

> *Megyn stops eating and looks at her mother.*
> *Carmel gathers herself together and wipes her eyes.*

Don't you worry about me. You just carry on with that butty.

> *Megyn nods and eats some more of the sandwich.*
> *They watch.*
> *She puts some half-eaten sandwich back on the plate*
> *and pushes it away.*
> *She drinks some more orange squash.*

Sarah Have you had enough?

> *She nods.*

Carmel I'll take her home. (*To Megyn.*) Let's take you home.

> *She goes to put her arm round Megyn but she moves away.*

Come on.

Megyn No.

> *Carmel steps back.*

Sarah (*to Megyn*) What is it? What's wrong?

> *Megyn looks at the floor.*

Maybe she's still scared. (*To Megyn.*) Are you scared?

Megyn thinks. Then nods.

Carmel (*hushed*) Don't be putting ideas in her head.

Sarah I'm not. Just look at her.

Carmel There's nothing to be scared of. Come on.

She doesn't move.

What is it?

Sarah Are you still frightened?

Megyn nods more forcefully.

Carmel (*to Sarah*) Oh look what you've started.

Sarah I know you haven't been outside for a while, but everything will be fine.

Sarah Maybe you should leave her here.

Carmel Enough of this now. She needs to come home.

Sarah Your mum's gonna look after you. Nothing's gonna harm you. You're safe now.

Megyn won't look up.

Carmel (*getting angrier*) You can't stay here any more. It's not good for you.

Sarah What is it you're scared of?

Megyn looks down at the floor.

If you tell us we'll be able to help, make it better.

She doesn't answer.

Is it the environment? What's happening to the planet?

Pause.

You can tell us.

They both look at her. She won't look up.
Carmel starts to well up. She can't look at Megyn any longer. It's all too much for her.

Carmel I can't . . .

She's standing near the open patio doors. She turns and runs out of the doors into the garden. She's gone.

Sarah (*under her breath*) That's all we need.

Sarah's not sure what to do.
   She sits down at the table near Megyn. Who's still looking down at the floor.

What are we gonna do, eh?

Megyn doesn't respond.

There's no one else about now. You can tell me anything you know . . . It can be just between us if you want . . . I think we've got quite a lot in common. Similar . . . If someone has done something to you. Or you've done something . . . It's better to let it out than keeping it all bottled up inside . . .

Megyn looks down at the table and grips her phone.

Is it your mum? (*With a laugh.*) We're all frightened of her you know. Are you scared to go home and be with your mum?

Megyn doesn't answer.

I know she can be a bit harsh . . . God, I get it in the neck from her all the time . . . And it may not seem like she's on your side, but she is . . . She's just got a funny way of showing she cares . . . Maybe you were just gonna stay here that first night or two . . . And then things just . . . You don't have to explain yourself . . . If it's all got out of hand you can put a stop to it now . . .

Megyn raises her head slightly. A flicker of interest. But Sarah misses this. She has an idea. She looks round to see Carmel is not near.

You know, if you're worried about going back home, being with your mum . . . You could come and stay with me for a bit if you want. It's just me there. All on me own. I've got a spare room. Could be fun. I'd love it. You could then come with me into school too. Shadow me. Get you out there in the world. It'd be like the old days when you were little and you used to come and play sleepover. We'd watch a film, I'd make popcorn . . . We'd have hot chocolate and . . . What do you think? Could be great.

Megyn shrugs.

Maybe not.

Sarah's phone pings. Megyn micro-flinches.

Oh, I'm sorry. I've just got to . . . (*She looks at her phone.*) No . . .

She puts her phone on the table.

We're living in crazy, uncertain times. It is a scary world out there. Or can be . . . Maybe that's not helpful . . . If I start thinking . . . about fearful things, the future, my life, it can all get out of control and eat you up . . . You've got to stay positive, optimistic. (*With a sense that she's trying to convince herself maybe more than Megyn.*) Things will get better. I really do believe that. I have to believe that. If I don't, then what have we got?

Sarah thinks for a moment. Almost drifting off into her own thoughts.
Pause.

I've been through some tough times. Yeah, yeah. It got so dark once I . . . They don't even know this. Me dad never knew. I took some pills. Some – well loads – and ended up . . . Gary, I don't think you knew him, found me just in time apparently . . . I just couldn't see a way through . . . So, you know I've been . . . too . . . I understand . . . Maybe I shouldn't have told you that . . . Things will get better.

Pause.

We've all got each other. What are we gonna do with you eh?

She gets up and looks out of the patio doors.

I can't see your mum . . . I think I should go and see where she is . . . That's the only way we're gonna sort this out. Will you be okay if I leave you alone for a moment?

Megyn nods.

Your nan's upstairs. I won't go far. Be dead quick. We'll sort this out.

Sarah picks up her phone and goes out into the garden through the open patio doors.

(*Off.*) Carmel?

Megyn is left alone.
    She sits with her head bowed. Still and quiet. Not sure what to do.
    Long pause.
    She looks up very slightly and listens out. It's silent. She then drops her head back down again.
    Pause.
    She then reaches across to take a crisp from the bowl. She eats it with tiny bites as she did before. Still with her head bowed. She takes another and eats it but less delicately than she did when everyone else was there. She takes another and eats it more confidently. She grabs a couple more and chomps away on them.
    She thinks.
    She lifts her head and slowly sits up – much less stooped. She's a little unsure as she does this.
    She sits up straighter and looks around the room.
    She listens out. Everything is heightened. Almost like she's using some of her senses for the first time.
    She's not sure how this feels and goes back to being slumped.
    Her phone pings. She quickly reads the message and sends a reply. Still half stooped over her phone. Almost immediately she gets a reply and a ping. Then another

ping in quick succession. She replies. Then sends another message for good measure.

She becomes engrossed in her phone. Swiping through different apps. Reading posts people have put up. Replying at great speed, two finger typing.

One message plays some dance music, she watches for a moment, then swipes it away. Another plays a section of Martin Luther King's 'I Have a Dream' speech. She watches for a moment, then swipes it away. Then the sounds of some girls fighting. She watches fascinated for a while, and then hurriedly gets rid of it.

Pause.

Then she comes to a halt and pushes the phone away into the middle of the table.

She tries sitting back up straight again. She does and it feels okay this time.

She tries to get up but she's feeling a little weak.

She stands up using a chair for support.

She takes in the room. Looking at it all afresh. It feels tiny and strange.

She listens out again.

A dog barks a few houses away.

She listens some more.

The sirens of a police car in the distance.

She notices the framed family photos next to her on the sideboard.

She looks at each one – almost like she's never seen them before.

She picks up a picture of Doreen's husband, the father of the family, and looks at it closely. Staring at it.

Pause.

She places it back on the sideboard but face down.

She stands still and looks down at the weird dress she's in. She half laughs to herself.

She thinks. And thinks.

It's all getting too much. She's angry.

Megyn No, no, no, no . . .

She punches her leg a few times.

A wave of something comes over her and she becomes panicky.

Her breathing becomes short.

She's about to tear up and cry. She's not sure what to do. Almost looking round for help.

She promptly picks her phone up from the table and starts scrolling through various apps. It seems to help her as her breathing slows.

She does this for a few moments until she's calmer.

She stops looking at the phone but keeps tight hold of it.

She hesitantly moves over to the patio doors, becoming more confident in her movement as she does. Standing taller.

She tentatively looks out.

She can't see anyone.

She moves to step outside but there's something holding her back.

She looks towards the sky and feels the sun on her face.

She closes her eyes and lets the sun beat down. A bird sings in a neighbour's garden.

Children can be heard playing in the distance.

Pause.

She opens her eyes and heads towards the kitchen.

Doreen moves about upstairs.

Megyn stops in her tracks.

She looks up and listens.

More movement above.

Doreen is now singing another Tina Turner song, 'Simply the Best', faintly to herself upstairs. She sings a couple of lines of the chorus.

Megyn smiles to herself.

She writes a quick text and sends it. Becoming a little stooped as he does.

Doreen sings a couple more lines of the verse, off.

Megyn listens out. A faint ping upstairs. This makes her smile.

Doreen stops singing.

Megyn stares at her phone, waiting for a reply.
Pause.
It pings. She reads the message and hurriedly texts a
response and sends it.
She listens out.
Pause.
A faint ping from Doreen's phone upstairs.
Pause.
Megyn's phone pings. She looks at the reply and smiles.
She then becomes engrossed in her phone again for a
moment. Scrolling and scrolling.
But she reads something she doesn't like. She becomes a
little anxious, then furious.

Stupid . . .

She hastily writes a message.
She thinks for a moment.
Writes some more and sends it.
She's still seething.
She writes another message. Almost muttering to herself
as she types.
She sends it.
She thinks.
She's still wound up.
She looks at the phone in her hand – almost with a look
of disgust.
She throws it across the room.
It lands on the floor by the sideboard.
She's still wound up.
She hits her leg again a few times.

Stupid fuckin' . . .

She looks down at the dress she's wearing and becomes
angry at it.
She starts pulling at the neck like she wants to tear it off
her.
She wants to rage at something else.

She grabs the table like she's about to flip it over.
She hears voices from the garden.
She freezes.

Sarah (*off*) You're gonna do as you're told for once and come back in . . .

Megyn is unsure what to do.

Carmel (*off*) Okay, okay . . .

Megyn rushes back to the seat she was sitting in.
She goes back to the stooped position she was in.
But that doesn't feel right.
She sits up more upright. But this doesn't feel right either.

Sarah (*off*) Come on. Enough of this now.

Megyn goes to somewhere in between – a little stooped and looking down at the table.
Sarah comes back in, followed by a very upset-looking Carmel.
Megyn looks up, seemingly timidly.

You've got nothing to worry about. Your mum just wants to say a couple of things.

But before she can speak, Doreen appears.
She's got a bright summer dress on and shoes with a bit of a heel.
She's getting her things together. Her handbag is on the sideboard.

Doreen I'm off now. It's good she's eaten. (*To Megyn.*) I'm glad you're feeling better . . .

Carmel You what? Is she?

Doreen (*to Carmel and Sarah*) She sent me a text, thanking me for the cheese sandwich. Saying it was nice.

Carmel Did she now?

Doreen She'll be better now she's out of that room. Now that's all over with.

Sarah You still going out? After everything that's happened?

Doreen Yeah.

A car beeps outside.

That's me.

She finds her handbag and takes out a small bottle of perfume. She gives herself a couple of sprays.

Looks like it's a lovely day out there. Lock the doors for me if you go out. T'ra.

Doreen puts on a pair of sunglasses and goes out through the patio doors.

Sarah (*to Doreen*) I don't believe you're . . .

Carmel Oh shut up.

Carmel tentatively makes her way over to Megyn.
Sarah spots Megyn's phone on the floor. She picks it up.

Sarah (*to Megyn*) What's your phone doing over here?

They both look at Megyn.

How did it get over here?

Megyn looks down at the table and shrugs.

Carmel It doesn't matter.

Sarah puts the phone on the table.
Megyn grabs it and holds it close.
Carmel comes down and kneels in front of her.
She's trying to keep herself together.

Is it me? Have I done this to you? Have I made you frightened? You frightened of me? You don't want to come home because of me?

Megyn won't look at her.

How could you be scared of your own mother? What's happened to me?

I'm sorry. I'm so, so sorry I've been such a horrible cow . . . Taking everything out on you. Will you come home and it'll all be different?

Megyn doesn't answer. She won't look up.
Carmel starts crying. She's desperate.

Sarah Your mum's really trying, Megyn.

Carmel I'll do whatever you want me to. You're my number one priority now. Please come back home. I'm begging you. I've missed you. My little baby. Megyn, I love you.

Megyn looks up at her mum. A genuine moment of connection.

What can I do to make you forgive me? I'm on my knees. I'll do anything for you to . . .

Megyn (*quiet*) Will you be nice to me?

Carmel cries.

Carmel Of course. Of course I will. I'm sorry. Tell me when I'm not being nice. You can say anything to me. Do whatever you want.

Megyn lifts her head and looks at her mum. She starts crying.

Oh Megyn. What are you crying for?

Megyn I'm sorry.

Carmel You've got nothing to be sorry for . . .

She holds out her arms.

Come here.

Megyn hesitates for a moment, and then moves into her mother's embrace.
They hold each other tight.

Everything will be alright. I promise.

Sarah wipes a tear away.

Sarah Oh God.

They break apart.

Carmel Will you come home? The house has been so empty without you there. So quiet. I've hated it.

Megyn doesn't move.

Please.

Megyn nods.

Come on, let's go.

Carmel stands up. She helps Megyn stand and supports her.

Sarah Is she going out like that? Wearing that?

Carmel Who cares? That's the last thing I need to worry about.

Sarah You gonna be alright? Do you want me to do anything . . .?

Carmel We'll be fine.

Sarah What should I do . . .?

Carmel You lock up here.

Carmel and Megyn make their way out through the patio doors.

Sarah See ya, Megyn.

Megyn smiles at Sarah.

T'ra.

Carmel T'ra.

Sarah is left alone.
She's not sure what to do.
She sits down at the table and looks at her phone.
Pause.

Then she looks at the empty room. It's very quiet.
She feels uncomfortable.

She goes over and looks out of the patio doors. She decides to close them and locks them shut. Leaving the keys in the door.

She goes through to the kitchen and we hear her locking the back door.

She comes back into the dining room and sits down.

She looks at her phone again but she's feeling rattled.

Looking around her almost like she's listening out for something.

She double checks she's locked the patio doors.

She peers out through the windows and decides to close the curtains.

She sits back down and looks at her phone.

She's unsure what to do with herself.

Her phone pings. She looks at it quickly but it's obvious it's not Simon. She doesn't reply.

She sits looking at her phone.

She gets up and goes through to the kitchen – gripping her phone in her hand.

She double checks she's locked the back door.

She heads out of the kitchen and goes to the hall that leads to the stairs.

We hear her going up the stairs.

She goes into Doreen's bedroom and closes the door behind her.

We now see Doreen's bedroom for the first time.

She climbs into Doreen's bed and sits up with the covers round her.

She looks at her phone, finds nothing there and puts it down on the bed next to her.

She's scared.
Blackout.
End of play.